The Power of Ethical Capitalism

Joe Zhankan Li

Published by Outlying Islands Publishing, 2024.

THE POWER OF ETHICAL CAPITALISM

First edition. November 15, 2024.

Copyright © 2024 Joe Zhankan Li.

ISBN: 979-8227338860

Written by Joe Zhankan Li.

Table of Contents

The Power of Ethical Capitalism

Why a Free Market Cultivates
Better Human Values

About the Author

Joe Zhankan Li, born in Guangzhou (China) and grew up in The Hague (the Netherlands), is an author, economics enthusiast and digital marketing professional. His writings often applying modern philosophy and history to economic theories. He is graduated from Erasmus School of Economics in the Netherlands, and he is also a Global MBA Graduate of National Taiwan University. He is the author of *Analysis of Income Inequality: Globalization, Technological progress and Money Supply* (China Times, 2017), published in Taiwan. He is now based in Frankfurt, Germany.

Dedication

To my Late Grandmother Shen Jie, the Love of My Life,
Whose Death Left a Hole in My Heart and Soul

謹以此書獻給我已故的外婆沈杰，
外婆是我每次回憶起童年時，第一個想到的人

Foreword: Capitalism and Humanistic Values

Chia-Wei Kuo

Dean, School of Professional Education and Continuing Studies,
National Taiwan University

Capitalism and humanistic values are often seen as fundamentally opposed. Capitalism requires a volatile and dynamic market economy, while humanism emphasizes stability and a harmonious social order. The young author Joe Zhankan Li suggests, however, that this traditional dichotomy needs to be challenged and reconsidered. By setting aside preconceived notions and examining the history of human civilization, we can find a more complex and dialectical relationship between these two systems – a relationship characterized by mutual dependency and reinforcement.

The core values of humanism began to emerge during the *Renaissance*, in 14th century Europe, when people started to break away from the constraints of the medieval church authority. Citizens and educated merchants in Europe began to focus on individual reason, freedom, and fairness, yet still couched within a structured social order. Three hundred years later, in the 18th century, Adam Smith introduced The Wealth of Nations, which emphasized the decisive role of market mechanisms and individual choice in resource allocation. Traditionally, these two ideas have been seen as irreconcilable. However, in modern society, the market mechanisms of capitalism have stimulated the intrinsic motivation of individuals to create value, benefiting society as a whole in the long run. Meanwhile, humanistic values provide essential guidance for the market order of capitalism.

Additionally, Joe Zhankan Li addresses several critical issues. For example, solely relying on subjective human rational design makes it difficult to perfectly reconstruct a stable and efficient economic system; institutional design has limitations. At the same time, the author highlights that capitalism has greatly expanded the range of choices for ordinary individuals and accelerated social mobility across different class strata, showcasing the value of capitalism. In the 21st century, countries with capitalistic system has demonstrated a more inclusive side, placing a stronger emphasis on fundamental social equity and integrating certain humanistic values. Therefore, it is reasonable to conclude that the two are interdependent and mutually reinforcing.

Examining the complex relationship between capitalist ideals and humanistic values is crucial for our comprehensive understanding of various aspects of modern society. This involves not only our understanding of economic development laws and economic systems but also whether the humanistic spirit can play a proper guiding role in contemporary social practice, ultimately steering our society toward greater prosperity, justice, and nobility. This book offers a new perspective, encouraging us to set aside prejudices, deconstruct traditional authorities, and re-evaluate capitalism and humanistic values.

Preface: Is Capitalism Evil?

I was born in Guangzhou, China in 1987, almost a decade after the *Chinese Economic Reform*[1] began. I have never personally experienced the era of the planned economy. For me, that period seems like a legend—everyone talks about it, but it was never part of my life. On one hand, the adults around me in my childhood were unanimous in their admiration for the positive changes brought by the Chinese Economic Reform, noting significant improvements in their material lives compared to the planned economy era.

On the other hand, when discussing capitalism, most adults would speak with disdain. Perhaps due to the deep-seated influence of communist ideology, people habitually associated capitalism with negative traits: evil, hostility, and decay. As a young man, I did not fully understand this, and as I grew older, I became curious about the differences between the Chinese Economic Reform and the previous planned economy period. To my surprise, I found that the core principles of the Chinese Economic Reform—such as the reduction of state control in favor of private enterprise and respect for market mechanisms—are characteristics of capitalism. I gradually realized that the conversations among the adults around me were filled with contradictions. The very capitalism they were criticizing was at the heart of the reforms they were praising.

At the age of twelve, before I completed elementary school, I immigrated with my parents to the Netherlands. Interestingly, even in Western Europe, where freedom of speech is valued, capitalism seems to be treated as somewhat taboo, and is rarely praised in public. In contrast, voices advocating for more equal income distribution and the protection of vulnerable groups via government intervention are much more assertive. In my high school history classes, the term capitalism was often accompanied by others such as economic crises, the survival of the fittest, human greed, and income inequality. A 2021 survey in the United States revealed that more than half of young people held a negative view of capitalism, and this trend appears to be increasing.[2]

It was only after entering university and joining the economics faculty that I began to gain a systematic understanding of capitalism. Arguably, capitalism is one of the most crucial pillars of human society. We must admit that, to date, capitalism is the most effective system for creating material civilization. In the realm of economics, capitalism's contributions to human society are countless. For instance, capitalism has increased production efficiency, significantly reducing the likelihood of future famines and lifting many out of poverty. It also allows individuals to seek purpose in life beyond mere survival, since more people no longer need to worry about basic needs such as food and shelter; instead, they can focus their energy on self-actualization and other meaningful aspects of life. The material prosperity brought about by capitalism has increased human mobility, enabling people to travel and work in other countries, thus broadening their horizons and continuously enriching the human civilization. These points are well-accepted in the field of economics, however, so they are not the primary focus of this book.

The ability of capitalism to generate material wealth is undisputed, but its most criticized aspect is its ethical shortcomings, which this book will explore. As previously mentioned, capitalism is often labeled as greedy, money-centered, and ruthless, and thus immoral. One example is that some left-wing supporters in modern societies disapprove of commodifying labor, which is seen as damaging to human dignity. However, if workers voluntarily offer their labor in exchange for salary to employers without coercion, and such employment allows both parties to achieve their goals, is not this voluntary agreement a win-win situation? Another example is the view that capitalism's encouragement of profit-seeking is immoral. Yet that profit often is the return capitalists earn for having added value to society or contributed positively. When business activities result in profit, it also drives future production by reinvestment, which will generate even more added value and create a positive loop of wealth accumulation. Achieving humanistic values through the promotion of virtue and charity is inefficient and unstable, making it unlikely to be implemented on a societal level.

The main distinction between modern and traditional societies lies in the fact that we no longer see material wealth as the only goal of societal development. Instead, we prioritize human-centered values such as democracy, freedom, equality, and rights, marking the boundary between modern and traditional societies. This means that a country's level of civilization is determined not by its wealth but by its respect for humanistic values. History shows that countries that value and promote humanistic values often have capitalism as their economic system. Conversely, countries without capitalism tend to be not only materially poor but also hotbeds of autocracy, theocracy, and authoritarianism. Although capitalism may appear chaotic, it has the power to reflect moral and humanistic values. Additionally, on a societal level, achieving humanistic values through capitalism is far more stable and natural than through religious faith, the promotion of virtues, moral education, or rational institutional design.

I do not believe that faith, praise, education, and propaganda alone can create a civilized and moral society. Instead, I agree with the Chinese philosopher Guan Zhong's saying, "When the granaries are full, the people know etiquette; when they have ample food and clothing, they know honor and disgrace". Only with a foundation of material prosperity can people be expected to uphold morality and humanistic values.

Capitalism is not a perfect system, but it is, like democracy, the least flawed system developed by human civilization so far. The essence of capitalism is freedom, yet it has always accepted and integrated critiques from egalitarian viewpoints, constantly evolving and improving to fit the morally diverse society of the 21st century. Every gain comes with a price. The freedom in capitalism is no exception, as it comes with the cost of risk and responsibility. Individuals must bear the consequences of their own choices. The freedom that people enjoy in capitalism does not mean they can be complacent. The core principles of a free market encourage individuals to make choices, innovate, take risks, and bear responsibility for their actions. However, there are those who wish to exercise freedom of speech and choice while condemning the intense competition of capitalism. They also expect society to rescue them without facing the consequences when their decisions fail to make them successful in free market. This reflects a tendency to avoid responsibility.

Human civilization progresses through the nurturing of values and ideas, not through material goods and profits. Paradoxically, values and ideas are most often realized when material abundance and profits form their foundation. Therefore, pursuing material wealth through capitalism is not evil; rather, it is a means to achieve higher humanistic values.

Joe Zhankan Li
5th November 2023,
Tokyo, Japan

Introduction: Do Capitalism and Humanistic Values Clash?

To the general public, capitalism and humanistic values often seem like two completely opposing concepts. When capitalism is discussed, many instinctively think of it as a system primarily concerned with making money. A research from the Institute for Economic Affairs (IEA) suggests that two-thirds of young Britons want to live under a socialist economic system and blame capitalism for economic crises.[3] Also majority hold of young adults hold negative view of capitalism in the United states.[4] Their common perception is that society is filled with individuals greedily accumulating wealth, and capitalists relentlessly exploiting the working class.

As a mechanism for coordinating economic activities and resources, capitalism promotes malicious competition and profit-seeking behavior in the free market, thus contributing to social division. In contrast, humanism is generally perceived in a much more favorable light. Humanistic values, such as freedom, equality, love, morality, and diversity, are universally acknowledged and admired, regardless of race or culture.[5] Consequently, capitalism is seen as representing the darker aspects of human nature, while humanistic values embody its positive attributes, making the two appear incompatible.

Nevertheless, capitalism and humanistic values are not only non-conflicting but are in fact complementary. A detailed examination of Western and global historical development, particularly post-Renaissance, indicates that capitalism and humanism have a synergistic relationship. It can even be asserted that the capitalist system is the foundation upon which humanistic values are built.

Without the economic framework provided by capitalism, humanistic ideals cannot flourish. To instinctively think that humanistic values and capitalism are mutually exclusive is to misinterpret the nature of capitalism.

The Rise of Humanism

Typically, we trace the origins of humanism to the Renaissance[6], which began in 14th-century Europe. Prior to the Renaissance, the Middle Ages were characterized by a period in which religion profoundly shaped people's thoughts and behaviors. During this era, individuals prioritized religious values, and norms over personal ideals, and desires. Religion guided people on the values they should pursueand how they should live. To uphold religious authority and social stability, numerous rules were established that defined right and wrong, and dictated ways of thinking. In medieval Europe, homosexuality was not accepted, the pursuit of wealth was seen as greedy and immoral, and personal desires were considered evil. These perspectives were closely linked to the dominant role of religion in medieval society. Similarly, in the East, traditional Confucian teachings during the same period in China led to similar societal conservatism. Before the advent of modern society, Chinese society was also marked by the oppression of women and conservative superstitious beliefs.

However, that traditional conservative society has long since passed. With the decline of religious influence in the 14th century, people began to reconsider the nature of society and life. Although Christianity seemed to provide people with a stable explanation of the world and a sense of purpose, as the European elite became more knowledgeable, religious explanations no longer sufficed. People's thinking began to change. The focus shifted from God and religion to humanity. These elites found that outside the religious framework, understanding the world through human values and experiences might better reveal the meaning of their surroundings. Additionally, the elites started to recognize that over a thousand years earlier, the ancient Greeks, before the rise of Christianity, understood the world through philosophy and humanism. Therefore, this intellectual revolution in the late Middle Ages was called the Renaissance, aimed at reviving the humanistic values and thinking methods of ancient Greece. In essence, humanism seeks universally desired values such as reason, freedom, equality, and justice.

The Renaissance brought about many changes that gradually appeared in various areas of society. Initially evident in the arts, these changes eventually spread to academia, politics, and nearly all aspects of society. For example, in the arts, religion ceased to be the sole subject, and figures in paintings, sculptures, and literature began to express human emotions like love, familial bonds, and greed. Meanwhile, the gradual decline of religious sentiment reduced many of the church's authoritative regulations. Previously, the church alone had dictated what people should and should not do. But with the diminishing influence of religion, people began to build society based on their human feelings and understandings. Many previously unquestioned beliefs lost their standard answers during the Renaissance[7]. As the Renaissance developed over several centuries, modern concepts such as democracy, market economy, and individual rights all began to sprout during the Renaissance. From that time, people began to see the dawn of modern civilization.

The emphasis on human values that emerged after the Renaissance has only become more apparent with time, and its influence extends into the 21st century. The humanistic ideals pursued during the Renaissance remain the universal values that modern society seeks to cultivate today. In summary, humanism emphasizes the importance of individual worth, without the need to submit to the authority of religion, politics, or any form of collectivism.

The Rise of Capitalism

The term "capitalist economy, " or "capitalism" appeared relatively late in history. Generally, Adam Smith, an 18th-century Scottish philosopher, is considered the father of modern capitalist economics. By the 18th century, the Renaissance had been influencing Europe for nearly 300 years, and the impact of Catholicism on society had significantly waned compared to the Middle Ages (before the 13th century). During the same period, the Enlightenment introduced ideas of freedom and equality, which began to take root in European countries.[8] Despite these changes, it is difficult to claim that 18th-century Europe had fully adopted modern humanistic traits. Even though the influence of Catholicism had diminished, royalty and nobility still existed, occupying the highest social echelons and holding privileges within their national economies. Consider two examples: First, prior to the 18th century, Europe's economic development was predominantly agricultural, making land the most critical resource. Most land was owned by nobles and the church, leaving landless peasants and artisans at the lower levels of society, creating a significant wealth disparity.[9]

Second, the dominant economic theory of the time was Mercantilism, [10] which prioritized national economic interests over public welfare. The goal of national economic development was to enhance the country's wealth and military strength rather than improve citizens' living standards. Economic policies included encouraging exports and restricting imports to accumulate gold and currency, thereby strengthening national economic power. Simultaneously, the government and nobility imposed heavy taxes on the populace, monopolized high-revenue industries, and controlled the import quotas of certain goods to maximize national and governmental interests.

From these examples, it is clear that the socioeconomic conditions in Europe at the time were still a significant distance away from achieving freedom and equality. However, Adam Smith's *The Wealth of Nations*, published in 1776, transformed economic theory. The book's central idea is that economic growth requires reducing government restrictions. Smith believed in the presence of an *"Invisible Hand"* in the market, which, when allowed to function without interference, enables individuals to specialize in their skills, thereby boosting efficiency and productivity through the division of labor. This, in turn, leads to overall market prosperity. The brilliance of the "Invisible Hand" is that while individuals act out of *self-interest*, this mechanism naturally steers the market toward prosperity without the need for government guidance or supervision.

By allowing people to pursue wealth according to their talents and interests, individual initiative is significantly enhanced. Adam Smith, now known as the father of modern capitalism, established the foundational principles of a market economy. His promotion of a free market and the Invisible Hand reflects the ideals of freedom, equality, and justice. Smith's reasoning suggests that rather than creating social hierarchies or concentrating wealth at the top, a society more suited to economic growth is one where everyone has the chance to compete in the market, own private property, and seek profits. However, a free market requires not just liberty but also a transparent and effective legal system to punish rule-breakers, ensuring fairness and justice. In a society where economic transactions are freely conducted, breaches of trust are inevitable. A fair and efficient judicial system ensures that those who fail to honor their commitments are penalized, allowing market participants to trade without fear of being deceived. According to Adam Smith, giving everyone freedom might seem disorderly on the surface, but the brilliance is that the free market drives individuals to maximize their earnings, naturally leading society toward increased wealth and economic balance where everyone is satisfied. Ultimately, everyone in the market benefits. Smith called this phenomenon, where order in the social and economic spheres emerges without government intervention, the "Invisible Hand".

After 1800, Western countries began to implement market economies, leading to the rapid growth of capitalism. The below chart illustrates the GDP over the last two thousand years, representing the total wealth created by humanity. Until 1800, the ability to generate wealth remained largely unchanged. The material wealth available to people in France around the French Revolution of 1800 was quite similar to that of the Gauls under the Roman Empire around 0 AD. However, post-1800, there was an explosion in human wealth and that wealth continues to grow into the present day. This surge was a result of the global adoption of free market economies, which provided individuals with the freedom to produce and create, thereby unleashing

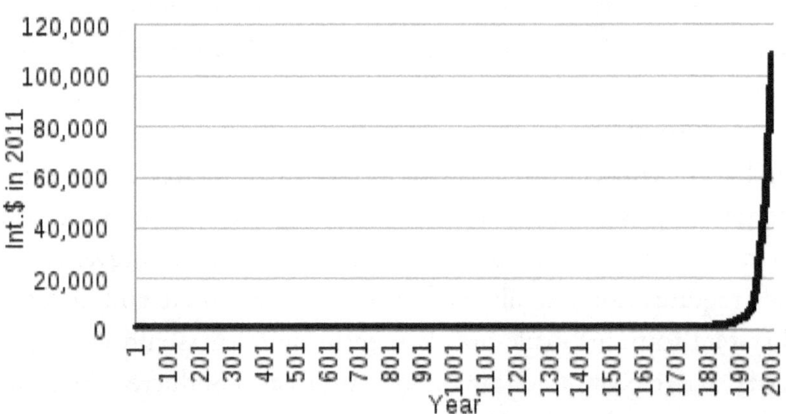

societal productivity. This shows that economic development is more effectively achieved by entrusting decision-making to the private market, thus maximizing wealth creation potential, rather than having the government dictate national prosperity.

Please note that while capitalism and a free-market economy are largely synonymous and interconnected concepts, they are not entirely the same by strict definition. A free market is characterized by decisions and transactions determined by supply and demand, [11] rather than government intervention. There are no external regulations dictating who can do what. Individuals in the market can freely compete and earn profits through production. The concept of a free market existed even before capitalism; in primitive times, before currency or in societies relying on subsistence farming, people still needed to exchange goods. Though in the underdeveloped economies of ancient times, both demand and supply were minimal, resulting in small markets.

Capitalism, on the other hand, refers to a system where private property rights are respected and inviolable. Owners of property or capital can invest to generate profits, which belong to them. Business decisions, such as what and how much to produce, are entirely determined by the free market. Adam Smith emphasized that all market decisions and transactions should be made freely and voluntarily by individuals, without any external coercion. Only in such an environment can the market grow and accumulate wealth. However, public authorities play a vital role by providing a fair judiciary and protecting private property rights, ensuring that every market participant can confidently produce and create wealth without fear of being deceived.

Clearly, a free market is an essential part of capitalism; they are interlinked, forming the basis of the modern economic system. Theoretically, a free market could exist without capitalism, [12] but in reality, without capitalism and respect for private property rights, a free market cannot flourish. Private property rights and profits drive the pursuit of wealth; only the promise of profit can motivate individuals to produce and add value to the market. Without the incentive of profit, a free market would hold little significance. Essentially, a free market thrives under a capitalist system, and conversely, a free market is an inseparable part of capitalism. Since capitalism and the free market share the same principles and economic foundation, and have many overlapping characteristics, these concepts will be used interchangeably throughout this book.

Humanism and Capitalism Are Complementary

It is worth noting that the core principles of humanism and the capitalist free market are grounded in universal values. If we consider humanistic values as the goal, then the capitalist system serves as the means and platform to achieve that goal. Humanism prioritizes human interests and values, emphasizing individual dignity and personal fulfillment, including freedom and equality. Similarly, the capitalist free market seeks to realize individual value. Historically, we cannot deny the significant role that capitalism has played in shaping modern society. In fact, capitalism does not oppose humanistic values; rather, it provides the foundation for achieving social freedom and equality. Both humanism and economics are centered on human nature and human desires, and capitalism is the economic system that best aligns with these humanistic values.

The free market respects each person's self-interest and does not force individuals to change that human nature. The capitalist system allows every individual in the market to freely engage in creation, production, and the pursuit of profit. Only with freedom can individuals be motivated to create wealth. Yet Adam Smith emphasized that freedom alone is not enough; equality is also a vital element of the free market. Every individual or enterprise in the market must have an equal opportunity to enter any industry or engage in any kind of production, without privileged classes monopolizing the sector. What a person does should be determined by their efficiency and productivity, not by their social status. The market determines whether entrepreneurs' efforts are meaningful; those who produce good products naturally gain profits as a reward. Essentially, every individual and entrepreneur in the market is equal. Those with good ideas who are willing to take risks and invest capital can enter any industry, without hinders from government or privileged class.

Furthermore, a fair legal system is essential to protect individual private property and rights. When disputes arise between parties in the market, society must have a fair and just system to resolve these conflicts. An unjust legal system would undermine the market's ability to create wealth.

In a free market, transactions are win-win scenarios for both buyers and sellers, meaning both parties gain from the exchange. Sellers profit by creating good products or providing excellent services that meet buyers' needs, or that offer them value. Since most market transactions are repeated over time, honesty in transactions with customers is the best strategy for long-term profit. When everyone in the market follows this logic and strives to provide value honestly, societal ethics naturally develop. The harder one works, the more competitive their products become, and the greater their profits. When everyone actively seeks to create value for others, ethical standards naturally emerge.

Importantly, capitalism also provides the general public with the means to protect their rights to freedom and equality, indirectly leading to the development of democratic systems. The establishment of democratic systems, except in cases like Japan or Iraq where it resulted from top-down implementation after wars, by the wars'foreign victors, usually arises due to the efforts and resistance of the lower strata of society. Initially, their demands are not the abstract concepts of freedom or rights, but rather the protection of their wealth. History shows that as capitalist economies thrive, the lower classes gradually accumulate wealth and become the middle class. To protect their wealth, the middle class demands more political freedoms and enshrined equal rights. For example, in countries like South Korea and Taiwan, democratic movements occurred after the economic takeoff and the formation of the middle class. Thus, the free-market economy becomes a means to achieve political influence and democratic rights.

The success of the Western Industrial Revolution and the wealth explosion over the past three hundred years have validated Adam Smith's theories. The triumph of the capitalist free market is rooted in its profound respect for human values, granting each market participant the freedom and equality to trade. Individuals with a desire for wealth work hard and earn it. Those with talent and capability receive higher returns in the market. The market system maximizes individual incentives to produce, enabling society to generate increasing wealth. Simultaneously, the free market respects diverse values and judgments, allowing competition within the same market. The market decides who is right based on who can generate more profit through their ideas and efforts.

Despite the imperfections of the free market system, such as income inequality and volatility, we should seek to reform rather than abolish capitalism in favor of a planned economy, which would lead to greater disaster than the imperfections of free market. Countries with Capitalist system acknowledge its flaws, and the free market has continuously evolved, integrating egalitarian elements, countries like Sweden and Denmark in Northern Europe are great examples of this. The redistribution of income through taxation in Western countries exemplifies this. These policies represent government efforts to make capitalist societies more inclusive of human values.

Humanism and Capitalism Contradicted?

Yanis Varoufakis, an Economics Professor at the University of Athens and former Greek Finance Minister, has publicly reflected on his involvement in managing the European debt crisis in 2015[13]. During this time, he keenly observed that while Western citizens live in a capitalist society, their understanding of this influential force is significantly lacking. Compared to their understanding of issues like immigration or healthcare, most people's understanding of the fundamental principles of economic matters is limited, often relying on the guidance of political elites.

Why does contemporary society largely perceive capitalism as conflicting with humanistic values? There are two main factors: the excessive increasingly widespread demonization of capitalism in western societies and the misunderstanding of the relationship between materialism and values.

Firstly, since the 19th century and the earliest emergence of left-wing ideologies such as communism, capitalism has been heavily demonized. Although there have been various reversals and corrections over time, this influence has continued into the 21st century. The most prominent example is Karl Marx and his work, *Das Kapital*. In this book, Marx criticized the capitalist system, asserting that the pure free-market system contains inherent contradictions that will ultimately lead to its downfall. Marx's inspiration for writing this book came from observing the poor working conditions and social injustices of the lower class in London, which he argued was caused by uncontrolled capitalist development. He proposed a new system, communism, based on *public ownership*, as an alternative.

It is important to note that the free market is not a perfect system; unchecked development can lead to income inequality, corporate monopolies, and economic instability. However, the capitalist free-market system requires reform and improvement, not the abolition that Marx suggested. After all, the free-market system is most effective in promoting economic production and wealth creation and aligns well with human nature and humanistic values. Fortunately, in the 20th century, only a few countries fully implemented communism. Most countries worldwide have retained market systems with modifications as their primary economic development strategy. Even so, Western mainstream society still overemphasizes the negative aspects of the free market, overlooking that capitalism is actually the cornerstone of modern society. As a result, many people instinctively react negatively to the mention of capitalism.

The second point I would like to address is the overly simplistic understanding that society often has regarding abstract values and concrete materialism. Many see humanistic values as purely abstract, noble, and virtuous, while capitalism is perceived as representing the more grim and greedy aspects of human nature. For instance, we typically consider love to be pure and noble, but when it is linked to money, it is seen as dirty and ugly. This binary perspective is, in my view, too extreme and unrealistic. Instead, I suggest that Maslow's *Hierarchy of Needs*[14] offers a more appropriate framework for understanding the relationship between material wealth and spiritual values. Maslow's hierarchy, originally developed as a psychological theory, categorizes human needs into five levels: physiological, safety, social, esteem, and self-actualization needs. While Maslow designed the levels to analyze an individual's psychological needs, it can also help explain the connection between financial materialism and spiritual values.

Self-actualization needs

Esteem needs

Love and belonging needs

Safety needs

Physiological needs

At the base of the hierarchy is physiological needs, which include basic survival requirements such as food, water, and other material necessities. Above physiological needs are the levels that involve spiritual values, not directly related to survival. Material needs, or fundamental human necessities, play a role in individuals' existence similar to the role of capitalism in society. We need an efficient system to create material wealth first. Once society's material needs are satisfied, we can then focus on higher-level spiritual needs. This explains why the countries with the richest cultural lives are often the wealthiest countries, too. Therefore, the pursuit of material wealth and the aspiration for humanistic values are not inherently contradictory but rather have a logical and complementary relationship.

Despite this, many wrongly believe that capitalism leads inevitably to rampant materialism and creates a culture of greed. This is a significant misunderstanding. Choosing capitalism or a free-market system as an economic mechanism can indeed efficiently drive economic development and generate material wealth, but this does not mean that material wealth is the ultimate goal of societal development. On the contrary, even within capitalism, the aim of economic and social development remains the promotion of humanistic values. Capitalism is merely a means to that end.

Both Eastern and Western cultures have long recognized that humans have an inherent capacity for love and empathy towards those around them and often act selflessly to meet the needs of others.

However, love and empathy are typically extended only to one's immediate circle. When dealing with outsiders, history shows that humans can be cruel, selfish, and indifferent. This aspect of human nature is generally viewed as unchangeable. As civilization progresses and becomes more global, cooperation among strangers becomes essential, and this self-interested aspect of human nature becomes an obstacle.

Before capitalism, elites in ancient societies implimented the moral education of the masses, often through religion or philosophical teachings. Western and Middle Eastern societies developed religions such as Christianity and Islam, while China created the Confucian system, all aimed at guiding people toward virtue and social order. While these methods had some success in advancing human civilization, their effectiveness was limited. This is similar to a modern company that promotes hard work through slogans rather than employee salary increases. Additionally, these moral teachings often lacked practical enforcement, leading to hypocrisy. For example, corruption occurred on a large scale throughout the Chinese Qing dynasty, even though all officials were trained in Confucian teachings, and pre-Reformation European priests preached morality while selling indulgences for profit.

The unique aspect of modern capitalism is its ability to bind morality with self-interest. It enables individuals to act with integrity and create value, even value that benefits strangers, while being driven by personal benefit.

Societies Without Capitalism

Is it possible for a country or society without a capitalist system to truly reflect humanistic values? To explore this, we can look at the communist governments that existed during the 20th century, such as Communist China and Soviet Union. Communists argue that allowing the market to develop freely only leads to economic disorder and increased wealth inequality. Additionally, communists advocate for public ownership of the means of production to liberate the proletariat and achieve true freedom and equality for everyone.

Communism is idealistic, but what were its practical outcomes? The Soviet Union, before its dissolution, and China, before its economic reforms, provide prime examples of the results of the communist society experiment. It can be said that these communist societies, which rejected free markets, achieved neither freedom nor equality. On one hand, these countries never implemented democratic elections, and speech and expression were highly restricted, limiting individual rights. On the other hand, the government assumed full responsibility for the distribution of resources and wealth to achieve equality. This conferred absolute power to the government, creating significant inequality between the state and the people. Moreover, historically, communist societies without a free market experienced widespread poverty and even famines (such as the one in Soviet Union the 1930s and the one in China late 1950s). In such environments, humanistic values were notably absent.

Economics as means, humanistic values as end goal

Many people today believe that economics is rooted in practicality and self-interest, representing profit calculations, while humanistic values stand for ideals and aspirations. They consider economic interests to be rational and morality often to be irrational, with no room for the coexistence of the two. When values and ethics are mentioned in economic discussions, they are frequently dismissed as insubstantial reasoning for an argument. It is as if economics and morality are opposites, with no interaction. This perception is fundamentally flawed.

The practical interests in economics should not be directly equated with money and material wealth. Few would agree that life's purpose is solely material enjoyment and financial gain. Individuals pursue what they consider to be important, based on their personal values. People often seem to work hard for money, but in reality, they see that money as the freedom to travel and see the world. Viewing economic issues solely in terms of material benefits without considering the underlying values leads to a shallow understanding of economics and potentially misleading conclusions.

I once read an economics story about a charity organization abroad that wanted to encourage blood donations and therefore offered financial compensation for each donation. They believed that financial rewards would increase the number of donors. However, contrary to their expectations, the number of donors decreased. Setting aside the ethical questions surrounding paid blood donations, economists explained that the original sense of pride in contributing to society was undermined by the "vulgar" act of receiving money. This is an example of how ignoring values and focusing solely on financial incentives can be counterproductive, even in a capitalist society.

While economists often use numbers or money to express benefits, this is nothing more than a simplefied way of thinking to describe the reality, and does not mean to suggest that all economic activities exist solely for monetary gain. For instance, on a microeconomic level, people enjoy coffee, but this enjoyment is subjective and difficult to measure, so economists use price as a standard unit to convey the coffee's value. On a macroeconomic level, people seek happiness, but since happiness is subjective, money serves as a convenient measurement unit. Thus, GDP was created to gauge economic strength, under the assumption that wealthier nations are happier (an assumption that remains open to debate).

Additionally, the importance of material wealth and benefits to society cannot be denied. Capitalism excels in efficiently creating wealth and enables individuals to provide value to others. Encouraging individuals to act in their own interest to do good has been proven to be a more stable than relying on traditional, religious, or doctrinal motivations, since all individuals must provide values to others in order to gain profits in a free market. History demonstrates that fostering moral behavior without economic incentive works within families or small groups, but at the societal level where cooperation among strangers is required, capitalism's capacity to generate benefits proves more effective in achieving humanistic values. Therefore, we should not confuse the means with the ends: capitalism is a means, while humanistic values are the goals we should aim to achieve in modern society.

Chapters of This Book

This book's chapters are dedicated to examining the relationship between modern capitalism and humanistic values. Chapter one delves into historical attempts to reform capitalism using rationality to achieve humanistic values. Following the Renaissance, the revival of ancient Greek traditions of rational and scientific inquiry extended into economics. Unfortunately, it is hard to claim that efforts to reform the free market over the past century have been successful. In fact, rigidly designed mechanisms to intervene in markets have led to many tragic outcomes.

Chapter two posits that capitalism is not at odds with humanistic values. On the contrary, capitalism and the free market are prerequisites for human morality. Humans are inherently self-interested, and this nature is difficult to alter. However, the capitalist system harnesses this self-interest, enabling individuals to create value for others. In capitalism, providing values for others becomes the only way to achieve self-interest.

Chapter three discusses liberalism. Individual freedom is central to capitalism and the functioning of modern society. Free competition plays a vital role in the free-market mechanism, driving innovation and progress. While some argue that free competition contradicts human nature, cooperation and mutual benefit are the prevailing dynamics in a free market. We should not overexaggerate the conflicts and competition among individuals in a free market. Additionally, capitalism supports democratic systems. Democracy and capitalism are based on many shared universal values. Historically, the democratization process in many countries was driven by citizens' efforts to protect their economic interests, leading to the pursuit of democracy. Thus, democracy and capitalism complement each other. This chapter also addresses the relationship between consumerism and capitalism. Critics argue that capitalism fosters consumerism, leading to materialism, moral decay, and a loss of freedom. However, this book contends that whether one falls into these traps depends on personal choice and character. Instead, capitalism provides more choices, and these choices are essential for expressing freedom.

Chapter four explores the issue of equality within the capitalist system. History shows that while capitalism can lead to income inequality, economic growth typically improves living standards and purchasing power for everyone. Often, those at the low end of the social spectrum gain the most. Moreover, Marx's theory of the upper class exploiting the lower-class laborers is flawed; the fact that workers may not receive satisfactory compensation does not necessarily mean they are being exploited.

Chapter five discusses how capitalism has continuously adjusted and evolved. By the 21st century, many egalitarian ideas have been incorporated into capitalism, and the concept of freedom has diversified and become more inclusive.

In chapter six, we look to the future and discuss whether society will continue to need capitalism and the free market system. Some argue that with technological advancements, governments might gather enough information and data to implement a planned economy or even communism. However, even with technological progress, our society is unlikely to move towards centralization. Instead, as the economy becomes more complex, greater individual freedom, innovation, and decentralization will be needed for growth. Thus, capitalism will remain necessary for future societies.

The capitalist system is fragile and must be protected. The principles of capitalism might at times conflict with politicians' interests, but if the capitalist system were to be destroyed or suffer significant setbacks, it could take decades to rebuild. In the worst case, humanity could face tragedies like those experienced in Communist China or the USSR.

1. Can a Designed Economy Achieve Humanistic Values?

Following the Renaissance in Europe during the 14th to 16th centuries, the influence of religion significantly waned in people's minds. Prior to the Renaissance, the Catholic Church dictated how individuals should live and what values they should uphold, with the bible serving as the ultimate standard for all things. People were expected to suppress their emotions and values to conform to religious moral codes. The Renaissance, however, shifted society's attention to human philosophy and values, gradually changing the standards for judging good from evil and right from wrong, to shared humanistic qualities rather than religious precepts.

The Rise of Rationalism

Despite the centuries that have passed since the Renaissance, the pursuit of humanistic ideals such as freedom, equality, and justice has not changed. How should humanity achieve these ideals? During the 17th and 18th centuries, the great thinkers of the Enlightenment encouraged societal progress and the pursuit of humanistic ideals through human rationality. This is not to say that rationality began only with the Enlightenment; ancient peoples also demonstrated rationality through their architectural marvels like the pyramids, the Colosseum, and the Great Wall of China. Humans have always used a combination of rationality, emotions, intuition, religion, beliefs, conjectures, and feelings to make judgments between right and wrong.

Rationality is often cited as the intellectual driving force of modern society. Yet most people's understanding of love and choice of life partners is based on emotions and intuition. Few rely solely on rational, objective standards such as wealth, social status, or income in matters of love. These examples illustrate that rationality is not the only criterion for human judgment, even today.

Why did rationalism gain such momentum in Europe after the Renaissance? The mainstream scholarly view attributes this to the philosophical traditions of ancient Greece, which, like Renaissance Europe, aimed to comprehend the world through human reason. Looking back at the history of Mediterranean civilizations two thousand years ago, it is evident that ancient Greece was a unique and fascinating place. After the Agricultural Revolution, Greece initially seemed to lag behind due to its poor soil, which hampered agricultural development. [15] Generally, the rise of ancient civilizations, such as those of Egypt, Mesopotamia, the Indus Valley, and China, was heavily dependent on a well-developed agricultural economy. The periodic flooding of rivers provided fertile soil, which greatly facilitated large-scale crop production. This agricultural development enabled these regions to support substantial populations and develop complex social structures. Ancient Greece was an exception; its geographic limitations prevented it from developing a highly advanced agricultural system. However, the serene Mediterranean Sea provided Greece with new opportunities, fostering robust commercial growth that expanded Greek horizons and shaped its social and religious structures differently from other Mediterranean societies.

Although ancient Greece had religions similar to those of contemporary Egypt and Persia, their influence was comparatively minimal. Generally, religion in ancient societies served to help rulers maintain social order by providing a belief system that encouraged people to live obediently and avoid independent thinking. Thus, most ancient states had strong religions that emphasized adherence to laws and discouraged free thought and skepticism. People's questions, doubts, and curiosity often faced the formidable barrier of religious authority, which deemed anything inconsistent with religious doctrine to be incorrect. Ancient Greece, however, stood out as an exception.

It had gods like Zeus and Venus, who possessed human emotions and desires, rather than being all-powerful gods with no imperfect human traits. This weaker religious influence allowed room for questioning and pursuing absolute truth through rational thought.

The term "Renaissance", meaning "rebirth", reflects the desire of Europeans at the time to emulate the ancient Greeks by reducing religious influence and understanding the world through their reason.

The Influence of Rationalism

In general, I concur that rationalism has been largely successful and has brought about numerous positive changes in human society, particularly evident in science and technology. Historically, individuals have employed rational thinking to understand the natural world, challenging entrenched social concepts and driving significant scientific advancements. Iconic examples include Newton's discovery of gravity, Einstein's theory of relativity, and Darwin's theory of evolution. These advancements in physics, biology, and chemistry have profoundly impacted the material conditions of human life. Without these pioneers' scientific breakthroughs, subsequent inventions like televisions, automobiles, and smartphones might not have been possible.

The most remarkable feature of science driven by rationalism is the discovery that the fundamental logic of nature can be mathematically described.[16] Moreover, nature's logic is universal and objective, applicable in all situations. For instance, water evaporates at 100 degrees Celsius and freezes at 0 degrees Celsius. This is a phenomenon universally observable and mathematically expressible. This perspective on natural phenomena exemplifies the post-Enlightenment scientific outlook.

Additionally, scientists frequently use concise mathematical formulas and models to capture complex and variable natural phenomena and physical knowledge. These equations are simple and elegant, effectively summarizing diverse phenomena and uncovering consistent truths in nature. Examples include Einstein's mass-energy equivalence formula[17] and Maxwell's Equations, [18] which unify the facts of electricity, magnetism, and light into the concept of the electromagnetic field.

This rational and objective mathematical approach has also influenced disciplines beyond the natural sciences. For instance, in psychology, the eminent Austrian psychologist Sigmund Freud was a pioneer in applying scientific methods to psychology. He analyzed patient case histories as data to uncover patterns explaining psychological processes (psychoanalysis).[19] Many of Freud's well-known theories, such as those on personality, the unconscious, psychosexual development, and childhood's impact on adult psychology, were derived using this rational approach. Although human psychology is difficult to quantify and many of Freud's theories are still debated and remain hypothetical, his renown stems from his methodological approach rather than from the provable accuracy of his theories.

In political science, in the period before American independence in the late 18th century, all political systems worldwide evolved naturally rather than by deliberate design. Systems such as the autocracy of the Chinese Ming and Qing dynasties, the theocratic rule of the Arab Empire, the power division in late medieval Europe, and the British constitutional monarchy all evolved from existing political realities. These systems were not designed from scratch but formed and were reformed gradually over time. While these systems were not necessarily the most rational for a country's culture and people, they were the most familiar. However, a notable modern exception is the United States. The American political system was created from scratch. From the Mayflower Compact to the Declaration of Independence and the U.S.

Constitution, the founding fathers used rational thinking to design a system suitable for their ideals, drawing on various European models.

The Impact of Rationalism on Economics

The rationalist movement also reached the realm of economics. In 19th-century Europe, many economists were dissatisfied with the dominant economic system, criticizing capitalism for being too laissez-faire[20] and disorganized, and thus failing to achieve principles such as freedom, fairness, and justice. These economists argued that humans should use rational thinking to design an economic system that optimally allocated resources.

The below table provides a brief overview of three main economic systems, categorized based on their stance toward market mechanisms and the necessity of governmental intervention. Adam Smith's classical theory, termed the market economy, advocates for market mechanisms as the most efficient way to run an economy, without the need for government involvement. The planned economy represents the opposite extreme, considering the market economy to be a system that causes social crises, one that should be replaced by a new, rationally designed system through governmental action. The mixed economy, positioned between market and planned economies, contends that the economy needs both market forces and human intervention to correct, adjust, and intervene where the market falls short. I will explain these three economic theories in more detail below.

	No market mechanism	With market mechanism
No or minimum government intervention	-	Market economy
With government intervention	Planned economy	Mixed economy

Advocacy for Rational Planned and Mixed Economies

The theories advocating for the rational transformation of economic systems are organized below into two schools of thought.

Planned Economy: Design by Rationality

The first school, represented by communism, advocates for a planned economy, also known as command economy, with Karl Marx's seminal work *Das Kapital* as its renowned theoretical foundation. The emergence of communism and planned economic thought is closely related to the Industrial Revolution of the 19th century. In London, at the height of the Industrial Revolution, Marx observed not only a booming economy, but also factories covered in soot, workers laboring for poor wages, and greedy, wealthy capitalists.[21] To Marx, the income disparity between capitalists and workers represented unjust exploitation that necessitated change. He believed that capitalism was the root cause of these inequalities. Marx pondered whether *laissez-faire* capitalism, which he viewed as a barrier to justice and a contradiction of humanistic values, could be overthrown and replaced with a rationally designed economic system that could realize humanistic ideals. This idea marked the inception of the planned economy.

The planned economy entirely rejects the market economy. Proponents of planned economies argue that capitalism, by allowing individuals to pursue wealth freely, unleashes human selfishness, resulting in economic chaos and income inequality, thereby destabilizing society. They believe that resources and means of production should not be allocated by the market but rather by the state or government through central administrative measures based on societal needs. In other words, economic activities such as the quantity of production, the type of goods produced, and pricing should be planned by the government rather than determined by market participants. They contend that implementing a planned economy would resolve issues like economic crises and income disparities. Communism's stance on the market economy is even more extreme than general planned economic thought, advocating for the abolition of private property and the communal ownership of all means of production, to be distributed by a government led by the proletariat.

Mixed Economy: market performs better with intervention

The other school of thought is known as the mixed economy, which combines the power of the market with rational government intervention. Advocates of mixed economies are much less extreme than those of planned economies and do not believe that market systems should be eliminated. Mixed economies recognize the strength of market mechanisms and argue that allowing individuals the freedom to produce and compete is the best way to develop the economy and achieve prosperity. On the other hand, unchecked capitalism can cause social injustices and other problems, so government intervention is necessary to mitigate these negative effects. The proposed model for a mixed economy is one where market mechanisms dominate, with government intervention playing a supporting role.

The most famous representative of mixed economic thought is Keynesianism, [22] which originated in the 1930s and is closely associated with economic crises. After the financial crisis in the United States in 1929, the economies of Europe and the entire world entered the Great Depression. According to classical economic theory, the market has self-regulating functions, and after a period, the economy will naturally recover and balance itself. For example, during a depression, individuals in the market become pessimistic and refrain from spending, causing businesses to lower prices. Once prices drop sufficiently, people will start buying again, increasing demand and stimulating supply, thereby restoring the economy.

Keynes did not doubt the market's ability to self-recover, but he identified many unacceptable shortcomings in the process as it would likely unfold in modern society. For instance, economic crises are a regular occurrence in capitalist systems, happening every few decades and causing ongoing economic anxiety. Additionally, Keynes's models showed that a free-market system inherently fails to achieve full employment, conflicting with the humanistic ideal of self-realization. Most importantly, Keynes argued that the market's self-regulation is too slow. The prolonged pain of depressions can erode public confidence and lead to social unrest, damaging the hard-won democratic systems in Western societies. Since the market's self-regulation is imperfect, Keynes believed that government intervention through administrative measures could help stimulate the market.

Many concepts we hear about in economic news today, such as monetary policies[23] and fiscal policies, [24] have their origins in Keynes's theories. For example, when the public is reluctant to spend, the central bank can use *monetary policies* to lower interest rates, making borrowing cheaper and encouraging consumption or investment. When high unemployment rates cause social unrest, the government can use *fiscal policies* to proactively invest in infrastructure projects like highways or railways, creating jobs and reducing public dissatisfaction.

A major commonality between the planned and mixed economy theories is their advocacy for using human rationality to reform or influence the free market system. If we consider the capitalist free market, where individuals freely compete to pursue wealth, as the natural state, then planned economies optimistically believe that human rationality can create a superior system to replace the market. In contrast, mixed economies argue that while our rationality cannot replace the market, it can guide and intervene in its operations to mitigate its adverse effects.

The idea of designing economic systems through human rationality had a significant impact in the 20th century, leading planned and mixed economies to become the mainstream approaches in most countries. Communist countries adopted planned economies, implementing them strictly through government directives. This was evident in the Soviet Union, pre-reform China, and other communist nations like Cambodia and Cuba. In the United States, the New Deal era, post-World War II, saw significant influence of mixed economic theories and Keynesian principles. Even into the 21st century, mainstream economics still holds that mild inflation can help achieve full employment and stimulate economic growth. Additionally, during economic downturns, fiscal and monetary policies are used to intervene in the market. The origins of these ideas and policies can be traced back to Keynes.

Can Rational Economic Design Truly Reflect Humanistic Values?

Rationalism has undoubtedly brought significant progress and improvements to humanity. Scientific advancements, industrial growth, and the digital revolution have greatly enhanced our quality of life. After the Enlightenment, people felt immense optimism about the future, driven by the achievements of rationality. It was believed that ignorance was the root cause of past misfortune and that continuous rational development would allow us to conquer nature and achieve happiness.

However, while the reverence for rationality persists into the 21st century, our outlook on rationality has grown more pessimistic as compared to a century ago. The Industrial Revolution massively increased productivity, but it also led to world wars with unprecedented weapons production and lethality. The internet and smartphones have offered unmatched convenience and entertainment, yet they have also introduced issues like social media anxiety, isolation, and indifferent interpersonal relationships. While democratic politics have flourished in Western societies, some countries have drifted further from democracy and freedom; authoritarian regimes are still prevalent outside the West. These instances suggest that while rationality can bring material and formal progress, it cannot directly satisfy humanistic values like freedom, fairness, and justice. Our earlier belief that rationality alone could secure happiness appears to have been overly optimistic.[25]

This reflection on humanity's rational endeavors extends to economics, as well. From the early 19th century to the late 20th century, the free-market economy, which emphasized minimal government interference and spontaneous order, was known as classical theory. This term suggested that relying solely on market mechanisms for national economic management was outdated and inefficient. For most of the 20th century, pure market-economy theories were not mainstream. Instead, planned and mixed economies, advocating for rational human intervention in markets, were more dominant comparing pure market economy. However, both approaches faced significant setbacks during the 20th century.

The Failure of Planned Economies

Let us take a closer look at planned economies. It is well-known that several communist countries, such as the Soviet Union and China, adopted planned economies in the 20th century. In a planned economy, the government decides what should be produced, how much should be produced, and at what prices goods and services should be exchanged. These decisions are implemented by state-owned enterprises. The idea behind planned economies was to nationalize all means of production to prevent the capitalist exploitation of workers and achieve absolute justice and fairness for all. Advocates of planned economies believed that capitalism is inherently unstable and prone to economic crises because it allows individuals to make free market choices. They argued that when individuals and companies produce based on their own expectations, economic crises occur when reality diverges from those flawed expectations.

Therefore, economic production decisions should be centralized and made by the government. Unfortunately, history has shown that centrally planned economies are doomed to fail, as evidenced by the experiences of the Soviet Union, China, Vietnam, Cuba, North Korea, and others. A review of these countries' histories under planned economies reveals widespread poverty, scarcity, and famine. These countries struggled to meet basic material needs, let alone uphold humanistic values such as freedom and justice. Some might argue that planned economies and communism achieved equality for all, but this equality was essentially universal equal poverty for all.

Economists who study communist countries have identified several reasons for the inevitable failure of planned economies in the history. These include the lack of healthy competition due to the absence of private ownership, the inefficiency of state-owned enterprises, and the government's lack of incentive for innovation. The common factor in these explanations is the belief that government and public authority cannot replace market mechanisms. In a free market, countless individuals make production decisions based on their observations and judgments. In contrast, proponents of planned economies believe that production decisions should be centralized. This means that the government, through administrative orders and state-owned enterprises, dictates how the economy should operate.

However, the government's resources are limited compared to the collective resources of individuals and enterprises in the market. The government cannot gather enough information to make informed production decisions. For example, deciding whether to open a Western-style burger shop or a Chinese-style buffet restaurant in a specific alley in the downtown, which requires understanding the local residents' preferences, is something a closed-door government cannot determine as accurately as the local community. Historically, when governments implementing planned economies could not obtain sufficient information, they often resorted to "guessing" how best to issue production orders, leading to numerous humanitarian disasters. A notable example is China's Great Leap Forward [26] in the late 1950s. As the 20th-century liberal economist Friedrich Hayek noted, no one can predict how many people will need white socks next year. In a free market, businesses closely monitor consumer preferences and can quickly adjust their strategies and products to meet changing market demands. In contrast, in a planned economy, production decisions and product adjustments are made by a small elite group, resulting in inefficiency, shortages, and mismatched demands.

Secondly, managers of state-owned enterprises often lack the drive to innovate and improve. For instance, if a local entrepreneur recognizes the profitability of opening a breakfast shop in their neighborhood, they will invest their own money and take on the associated risks. If the business fails, they know they will bear the loss. Consequently, the owner will make every effort to manage and innovate to achieve profitability.

Moreover, with multiple vendors often competing in the same market, success requires significant effort and intelligence. However, in a planned economy, production and services are determined by state-owned enterprises, where decision-makers are primarily bureaucrats. Generally, government officials are tasked with executing administrative directives rather than generating profit. If the order from above is to produce butter, the state-owned enterprise's primary objective is to meet the production quota for butter within the allocated time. Additionally, with typically only one state-run producer per product, there is no competition in the market. As a result, aspects such as marketing, quality, and customer service are not priorities, and there is no incentive for improvement. This explains the generally low productivity in communist countries that adopt planned economies.

Moreover, the initial communist aspirations for freedom and equality are notably absent in the planned economy system. Firstly, government and public authority control over production significantly restricts individual choice. As mentioned earlier, the government lacks the ability to understand market needs, leading to low productivity and shortages. The essence of freedom is choice.

However, governments with planned economy system, determine what is produced in the market and limit the choices for people.. Government officials, working in isolation with data and assumptions, cannot meet everyone's needs. Additionally, the premise of planned economies is that unrestricted free markets create societal inequality. However, in practice, planned economies have resulted in an equality of poverty and material scarcity. Furthermore, the nationalization of production resources grants excessive power to the government, creating a significant imbalance between the state and the populace. Thus, equality, whether in terms of material wealth or opportunities, has never been achieved in planned economies.

The Failure of Mixed Economies

Let us take a closer look at mixed economies. While acknowledging the market's ability to create wealth, mixed economies also recognize the side effects and significant deficiencies of the free market. Supporters firmly believe that human rationality can be employed to enhance or reform the market. In the first 50 years of the 20th century, this blend of market forces and human rationality was widely accepted. At that time, the prevailing economic wisdom credited President Roosevelt's New Deal, and Keynesian economics, with rescuing the U.S. economy from the Great Depression. During the Depression, when unemployment was rampant, it was believed that the government could use fiscal policies, even if it meant going into debt, to create jobs, reduce unemployment, and maintain social stability.

Moreover, when consumption and investment were insufficient to quickly recover the market, public authorities could intervene through the central bank by lowering interest rates to reduce borrowing costs and stimulate the economy. Essentially, the central bank could lower interest rates to make borrowing cheaper, encouraging people to take risks, spend, and invest. Simultaneously, lower interest rates would make saving less attractive, thereby promoting investment and spending. These two main market intervention techniques, derived from Keynesian economic theory, are considered fiscal policy: proactive government investment and monetary policy in which central banks adjust interest rates and money supply. The central idea is that instead of leaving economic development entirely to the disorderly market, humans can use rational intervention to make the market economy more efficient.

Mixed economies have significantly influenced global economic policies throughout the 20th century, and remain a central economic theory into the 21st century. From the late 20th century onwards, rational economic policies aimed at market intervention have become more prevalent. However, the negative side effects of such public interventions have exposed the flaws of mixed economies. Here are two examples of government intervention failures.

First, consider the stagflation phenomenon in the United States after the oil crisis of the 1970s. [27] At the time, it was believed that economic development depended heavily on future expectations.[28] Optimism in the market would encourage spending and investment, with prices serving as an indicator. Rising prices, indicating strong market demand, were thought to foster optimistic expectations, making mild inflation beneficial. This inflation could be managed through monetary policy by increasing the money supply, theoretically ensuring long-term economic prosperity. However, during the oil crisis, rising oil prices drove up the cost of other goods, while incomes did not rise accordingly. Despite the Federal Reserve's efforts to stimulate the market by expanding the money supply, the economy remained stagnating. This resulted in the coexistence of inflation and economic stagnation—stagflation.[29] The experience of stagflation in the 1970s shattered the myth that inflation could improve employment rates and stimulate the economy, and the belief that government intervention could resolve any economic downturn.

During stagflation, both expansionary and contractionary policies proved ineffective. Tightening monetary and fiscal policies to fight inflation would worsen an already depressed economy, while expansionary policies to stimulate the economy would lead to runaway inflation and potentially hyperinflation[30]. The stagflation issue stems from imported inflation[31] driving up the prices of other market goods, eroding economic productivity. Producers facing rising costs and an economic downturn may find it unsustainable to continue operations, leading to more business closures and bankruptcies. Addressing phenomena like inflation, economic recession, and stagflation requires restoring market confidence and productivity—something that cannot be achieved through counterproductive government policies.

Similarly, in Japan, following the signing of the Plaza Accord in 1985, [32] the Japanese yen appreciated rapidly. Japan quickly shifted from a low-yen-dependent, export-oriented economy to one that actively invested overseas. This increase in overseas investments brought significant wealth and GDP growth to Japan but also had substantial domestic side effects. The outflow of hot money due to foreign investments negatively impacted domestic consumption. Additionally, factories that once exported Japanese-made products began relocating abroad, adversely affecting domestic employment. To counteract the negative effects on employment and consumption, the

Japanese government initiated infrastructure investments to maintain domestic employment and consumption levels. They developed numerous infrastructure projects, including airports, railways, and municipal buildings. Unfortunately, many of these infrastructure investments had low utilization rates, resulting in unrecouped investments. Moreover, the capital for these projects was borrowed, leading to Japan's high national debt, which continues to be among the highest globally in the 21st century. To stimulate the economy, the Bank of Japan aggressively lowered interest rates and expanded monetary circulation, with much of the new currency flowing into real estate, creating a bubble. The bubble burst in 1991, causing the Nikkei index and property prices to plummet, leading to Japan's two "Lost Decades"[33] of deflation and stagnation. The mistakes made by Japan's central bank highlight the criticisms of mixed economies and government market intervention.

In addition to the questionable effectiveness of mixed economies and market intervention policies in stimulating the economy, they have faced criticism regarding social values and ethics. From a fiscal policy perspective, it is essential to recognize that the government does not create wealth; all fiscal expenditures come from taxpayers. The notion that government-led investments are more efficient than those made by individuals in a free market is unfounded, since the government is not able to find out the needs of everyone, to determine where the investments should go.

Furthermore, when public authorities actively intervene in the market through government spending, they often choose to invest in enterprises or projects deemed most capable of influencing the economy. For example, after the collapse of Lehman Brothers during the 2008 financial crisis, the U.S. government intervened to support other large, financially distressed investment banks. From the government's perspective, aiding large investment banks on the brink of collapse was the most effective way to stabilize the market and preserve jobs. However, this logic is flawed and dangerous. Essentially, the more an enterprise borrows, grows, and mismanages its business, the greater the likelihood of receiving government bailout. This approach is fundamentally unfair.

A Free Market-Driven Approach Is more Moral

Both planned and mixed economies historically exhibit a common trait: they often reverse the objectives and means of economic development[34]. Observing the flaws in classical market economies and capitalist systems, earlier thinkers sought to reform economic systems through their wisdom and rationality. While their intentions were undoubtedly noble, well-meaning ideals can sometimes yield the worst results.

The ultimate goal of economics is to enhance human well-being and happiness, with concepts like material wealth, wealth distribution, and GDP serving as the means to this end. In a planned economy, the government attempts to replace market mechanisms with a state monopoly on production, aiming to create a fair society. However, this often results in widespread poverty, where everyone is equally deprived. When basic material needs are unmet, and people face hunger, such a life is far from happiness and human values. Such impoverished equality is meaningless.

Mixed economies also risk reversing goals and methods. Neoclassical economists believe they can deconstruct every market operation and individual decision through mathematical models. They argue that by addressing problematic areas, they can resolve many of the free market's inherent flaws. While they recognize the market's self-correcting ability through price adjustments, they believe government interventions can achieve quicker and more direct results. Unfortunately, human intervention in the free market often exacerbates the problem, creating with market disorder and instability..

Issues that Arising from Market Intervention

National fiscal policy aimed at economic development and GDP growth serves as a prime example the flaws of market intervention. GDP, or Gross Domestic Product, [35] is a key measure in contemporary economics. It represents the total value of goods and services produced within a country in a year and is often used as a standard measure of economic strength: a higher GDP indicates a stronger economy. However, such emphasis on GDP can be misleading, confusing economic goals with means. In simple terms, GDP is the sum of a nation's consumption, investment, government spending, and net exports.

This definition might suggest that a country's ultimate aim is to maximize GDP. But is this truly the objective of economics? Adam Smith in the 18th century suggested that economic development should enhance national wealth and citizen happiness. Unfortunately, increasing investment and government spending do not directly translate to that key second piece, citizen happiness. Instead, consumption is more directly linked to citizen happiness, while investment and government spending are tools to achieve future consumption. Using borrowing or government spending to artificially boost GDP as a national development goal misplaces priorities[36]. Furthermore, governments often incur debt to fund their expenditures, leaving the repayment burden to future generations. Economic development should strive to enhance the well-being of citizens, not focus solely on economic metrics that can impose societal burdens.

Another example of market intervention is when central banks use monetary policy to influence the economy, a long- criticized practice by Classical and Monetary economists. Modern economic theory suggests that by increasing the money supply and lowering interest rates, borrowing becomes cheaper, encouraging people to spend and invest, thus helping the market recover during economic downturns. Later, the central bank wil raise interest rates again to pull excess money out of circulation and restore the money supply to normal levels, thereby regulating economic cycles. However, these policies, known as *"Quantitative Easing"*, [37] come with serious social side effects, one of the most significant being the worsening of inequality[38]. When the money supply increases, there is more money chasing the same amount of goods and services[39], which naturally leads to higher prices, a phenomenon known as inflation. It is important to note that new money is introduced into the market through loans, and typically, wealthy people and high earners access this new money first. Increasing the money supply does not lead to the immediate onset of inflation, therefore the wealthy can borrow and invest during that lag time when prices are still low. By the time the new money[40] reaches lower-income groups, prices have already risen. This pattern was observed after the 2008 global economic crisis, where wealth inequality increased worldwide, linked to the monetary policies implemented post-crisis.

The Core of Economics Is Human Nature

We must understand that the core of economic operations lies in human nature. Whether it is economic growth or recession, inflation or deflation, or the ups and downs of the stock and real estate markets, they all fundamentally depend on people's expectations of the present and future. Essentially, when we say the economy is bad or in a depression, we mean that society is pessimistic about future economic conditions, leading to a reluctance to spend or invest, which stalls money circulation. Both planned and mixed economies aim to reshape economic operations through rational human intervention and public authority, aiming to change economic expectations through government policies. In my perspective, this is too radical. Setting aside the question of whether it is possible to change people's thoughts and expectations, even understanding human behavior is extremely difficult. It is well known that human behavior is often driven by emotions and irrationality. People continue to gamble despite knowing the high odds of losing, and during economic crises, we often see investors panic-sell assets due to the influence of others. Some luxury consumption behaviors also defy basic economic principles, such as when higher prices lead to higher demand. These behaviors are hard to call rational.

In fact, due to the complexity of economic societies, modern economics often simplifies economic phenomena into mathematical models with basic assumptions for analysis[41]. One common assumption is that everyone in the market is rational and acts in their self-interest with strong computational abilities. If this were true, controlling or intervening in the economy might be feasible. However, as discussed earlier, human economic behavior is filled with irrationality, and even with advanced economic policies and intervention tools, we cannot avoid crises like the 2008 financial crash.

Another point where planned and mixed economies diverge from human nature is their macro-level approach to understanding market demand. Planned economies rely on the government's ability to accurately predict market demand and, by monopolizing all means of production, produce the required goods and services. The focus of planned economies is to control the economy through public authority to achieve fairness; economic growth, product variety, and freedom of choice are secondary considerations.

Mixed economies, on the other hand, allow the government to control total demand through market regulation. For example, during a recession, when spending is low, Keynesian economics suggests that the government invest in or subsidize certain industries or that the central bank lower interest rates and increase the money supply to stimulate demand. These policies operate on the belief that, although market demand cannot be precisely predicted, it can be stimulated through government intervention. If I initially only needed a bicycle, government subsidies and low-interest rates might encourage me to spend more or take out a loan to buy a better one or add more features. From a mixed economic perspective, continuous economic growth is essential to ensuring people's happiness.

In contrast, classical capitalist free-market economics views demand and growth differently. Adam Smith, the father of capitalism, argued that economic growth is driven by supply, not demand[42]. This is the opposite of mixed economic theory. According to classical market theory, economic growth comes from the supply side, such as increased productivity, efficiency, and quality. Innovation and progress are the sole drivers of economic development.

The evolution of smartphones is a clear example. Before 2010, the main function of mobile phones was making calls, and other functions like gaming and texting were secondary. With limited functionality, few people would have spent over $200 USD on a phone. However, smartphone innovations transformed phone functions. After smartphones were introduced, phones became devices for watching videos, browsing the internet, and taking photos. It was this breakthrough in phone innovation that led people to spend more money on them. From the market economy perspective, discovering people's needs through innovation is the only way to achieve economic growth and social well-being. Conversely, without innovation and progress, there should be no economic growth.

Economic growth driven by innovation and progress to meet demand is the most natural and beneficial for social welfare. This approach contrasts sharply with planned and mixed economies. Planned economies do not prioritize progress, product quality, or economic development; they assume that government control can achieve income equality, prevent exploitation, and avoid instability, thus ensuring a happy society. However, as discussed, history shows that such models often lead to poverty. Mixed economies argue that demand can be created and managed. But if we scrutinize this, do increased government spending, more subsidies, higher money issuance, and lower interest rates genuinely lead to economic prosperity? No, a nation's wealth primarily depends on its productivity. A country's ability to produce necessary and high-value-added products is key to its wealth.

Those who advocate for market intervention through public authority generally aim to design a more humane society that promotes happiness, freedom, and equality. Unfortunately, they often overestimate their rationality[43]. Planned and mixed economies may solve immediate problems and achieve short-term goals, but they tend to ignore long-term consequences. Planned economies focus on equality and restrict individual and private enterprise production, leading to long-term scarcity and poverty, hindering economic growth and social welfare. Mixed economies, while focusing on economic growth, also believe that such growth can be artificially created. Government-stimulated demand might produce short-term growth, but it does not represent technological advancements or efficiency improvements, which can have severe long-term side effects. Government investment and spending effectively reallocate market tax revenues, reducing choices for individuals and enterprises. Additionally, expanding the money supply through central bank policies involves borrowing from the future, increasing inflation. Such economic growth is illusory and does not meet the people's true needs.

The Free Market as a Tropical Rainforest

Planned and mixed economy often consider market as a machine. But instead of a machine, I prefer to compare it to a tropical rainforest. A tropical rainforest is not designed by humans, rather it is built by all the plants and animals within it, from scratch. None of these organisms understand their specific contributions to the ecosystem, but through generations of survival efforts, the rainforest takes shape. As self-appointed stewards of the rainforest, humans naturally desire its flourishing. However, since the rainforest is not a human design, we cannot fully grasp the roles of each plant and animal. Making arbitrary changes to species can disrupt the ecological balance, causing unforeseeable harm. Unless there is a disaster like a wildfire affecting all life forms, the best way for humans to manage the rainforest is to avoid intervention and let it develop freely. No human can better understand the needs and values of the rainforest's flora and fauna than they do themselves.

Financial journalist Greg Ip, in his book *"Foolproof"*, [44] categorizes those who think about economic mechanisms into two groups. The first group, economic engineers, utilize all available knowledge to design or create systems that make the economy more stable and secure. The second group, which Ip calls economic ecologists, remain in awe of the market and the complexity of human nature and the environment. Unlike engineers who aim to design economic systems, ecologists respect the natural market mechanisms. They are skeptical of attempts to engineer the market, believing that it is impossible to manage every detail of the market due to its complexity, so excessive intervention causes more harm than good. They advocate for preserving the market's natural operations to create greater wealth. I find Ip's analogy very appropriate.

Human nature is too complex, and the free market is too intricate. History has shown that human rationality cannot replace the market, and short-term benefits of market intervention are only temporary, leading to long-term side effects. I hope readers will consider the power of market mechanism, allowing the market to innovate and regulate itself to achieve more stable long-term economic development, enhancing the welfare and happiness of the populace.

2. Can Capitalism Show Humanistic Morals?

With the rise of leftist ideologies like socialism in 20th century, capitalism and the free market have been broadly viewed as economic systems that reveal the darker side of humanity in mainstream discourse in the western society. Mention capitalism, and people often think of capitalists who pursue personal gains at the expense of the broader societal good, neglecting noble human values.

However, this view represents a misunderstanding of capitalism and the market economy. A deeper examination of the market shows that, in reality, the free market not only avoids amplifying humanity's dark side but allows individuals to pursue their own interests while achieving shared humanistic values. Today, in the 21st century, it is apparent that the countries most capable of reflecting humanistic values are those practicing capitalist free-market economies.

These nations, such as developed countries in western Europe and Northern America, have robust welfare systems, democratic governance, and vibrant communities and organizations. They uphold universal values such as freedom, equality, and democracy. In contrast, some communist countries that promoted equality and state-owned enterprises while rejecting capitalism have histories filled with humanitarian tragedies, [45] and freedom and equality were never truly realized. Thus, the argument that capitalism is anti-humanistic cannot be invalidated by the practices of communist countries.

Human Beings Are Naturally Self-Interested

We must recognize that human behavior is driven by an individual's personal goals and pursuit of happiness. Adam Smith termed this as self-interest. While some might consider prioritizing one's own interests as selfish, it is in fact an inherent human trait, and there is no need to be ashamed of it. In his *Theory of Moral Sentiments*, Adam Smith did not mean that humans only care about their own interests to the detriment of others' happiness. He suggested that while people prioritize their own interests, they also care about the happiness of those around them, and that their level of concern depends on their proximity to others. We care for and share resources with those close to us, such as parents, partners, or children. Naturally, we might also help more distant neighbors in times of need, but to a lesser extent than close relatives. The concept of proximity to others is subjective and varies from person to person; some may even value their pets more than their parents. But understanding these theories of self-interest and the influence of proximity on concern for others helps explain why developed countries pay limited attention to distant, impoverished African nations, yet some individuals are willing to risk their lives to save strangers when they see an emergency happening right in front of them.

If humans are inherently self-interested and prioritize their own benefits, how does this shape societal development? Initially, before advanced economic systems were established, human interactions were driven by a Darwinian mentality. Before modern economic frameworks emerged, production and economic exchanges mainly occurred among close-knit groups, such as families and tribes. The term "economics" comes from the Greek word *"Oikonomia"*, meaning household management. Within these close relationships, cooperation and mutual support were possible. However, when dealing with strangers, especially during conflicts, humans' self-interested nature often led to fulfilling needs through plunder, war, or even killing. For example, before entering modern civilization, wars frequently occurred among various European tribes such as the Celts, Anglo-Saxons, and Vikings. Even into the 20th century, conflicts between African tribes were often reported in the news.

This Darwinian mentality explains why early human societies were slow to develop. Small social circles and distrust of outsiders prevented cooperation with strangers. From a modern perspective, this self-interest-driven survival model had two significant drawbacks. First, distrust of strangers hindered the exchange of ideas and technologies, slowing social and economic progress. Second, frequent violence and wars created extreme social instability, impeding civilizations' development.

Economist Dan Lavoie terms economic operations before the free market as *"traditional economics"*[46] . Lavoie explains that traditional economics involves activities governed by customs, religion, habits, and unwritten rules. These traditions and rules are the accumulated wisdom of ancestors, passed down orally over generations. Consequently, each village or tribe had its own economic rules and logic. Without unified market rules, economic activities tended to be conservative. The ancients believed that adhering to their villages' methods ensured survival and met their interests. They often avoided trading with strangers, with their differing trade rules and the risk of cheating. This explains why our ancestors were not skilled in cooperating with strangers in traditional economies, which stunted economic and civilizational growth.

Roles of Religion and Moral Teachings

Historically, ancient wise individuals have recognized these issues and attempted various solutions. In the West and the Middle East, religious institutions have served as a significant example of guidance for large-scale social interactions. Catholicism, Protestantism, and

Islam all promote doctrines of equality and mutual love among followers, aiming to maintain social harmony. Similarly, in ancient Eastern societies such as China, Confucianism sought to stabilize society through the teachings of Confucius and Mencius. Confucius emphasized benevolence, while Mencius promoted compassion, both advocating for altruism, much like Western religions did.

However, despite the positive moral effects these religious doctrines and Confucian teachings had on ancient societies, their influence was limited and could not achieve genuine altruism and humanistic values. The key issue is that neither religion nor moral instruction can solve the problem of human self-interest. Whether it is Christianity or Confucianism, the demonization of human selfishness and the promotion of universal love only lead to hypocrisy. Most people appear to respect these doctrines and profess their love for others, but when conflicts of interest with strangers arise, deception and even violent confrontations are common. The major flaw of Christianity and Confucianism is their attempt to change human nature through rigid rules. We must accept that, regardless of the methods employed, human beings cannot fundamentally change their self-interested nature.

Free Market Works Better to Promote Goodness

As humanity entered modern society and adopted capitalism, we seem to have found a more effective solution to the issues discussed earlier: the market mechanism. The ingenuity of the market model is that it does not seek to change human self-interest. Instead, it allows individuals to pursue their own interests while simultaneously benefiting others. In the capitalist system, people must create value for others before they can earn profits for themselves. This win-win outcome is a natural result of the capitalist market system.

As previously mentioned, the "invisible hand" of the free market regulates the economy. Adam Smith's original idea was that when society removes all economic restrictions and allows individuals to freely pursue wealth, people will naturally strive to produce and innovate. As a result, the market will be filled with more goods and services that people need, leading to more frequent exchanges of goods and money, and consequently, economic prosperity. This entire process requires no intervention or regulation; by allowing individuals to pursue their economic activity freely, the market will naturally accumulate wealth. This logic applies not only to material wealth but also to moral and humanistic values.

People also Consider Others in the Free Market

Firstly, let us consider why people consider others' interest in a free market. To achieve happiness and profit, individuals must evaluate their environment and decide which products and services to offer. The fundamental requirement for selling one's products is that one must provide value to others and bring them happiness. For example, if a restaurant owner creates delicious dishes through their effort and talent, and customers are willing to pay for these dishes, it shows that the owner has provided value. On the other hand, if an entrepreneur produces a useless product, they will not create value for others, and no one will buy such a product. Thus, to achieve personal happiness, one must first provide value and happiness to others. In other words, under capitalism, self-interest and considering others' needs can coexist; in fact, one could say that in a market system, self-interest requires consideration for others.

The Free Market Encourages Honesty

While achieving self-interest and consideration of others' needs, honesty among market participants is crucial and fundamental to the capitalist system. In pre-capitalist societies, where the rule of law was not well-established, dishonesty often occurred in transactions between individuals or companies. Sellers would highlight their products' and services' virtues to attract customers. However, better quality meant higher costs and lower profits. In the absence of strong legal frameworks, many chose dishonesty, exaggerating their product quality.

The free market encourages honesty by its very nature. Since everyone can freely produce and trade, multiple sellers will exist for buyers to choose from. When buyers have the freedom to choose, sellers can only maintain their business long-term by being honest. Ensuring product quality and fair pricing guarantees returning customers. If sellers deceive buyers with poor quality or overpricing, buyers, once deceived, are unlikely to return. While dishonesty might bring high short-term profits, it is unsustainable in the long run. In addition to the market mechanism, an effective legal system to punish dishonesty further enhances market efficiency. Although honesty is crucial for long-term gains, some business models might not require repeat transactions with the same buyers, making one-time exploitation an option.

Restaurants in tourist locales are an example. Tourists, unfamiliar with local prices and tastes, are susceptible to overpriced meals. Since most tourists do not revisit the same place, restaurants can rip them off without facing the repercussion of losing potential repeat customers. An example is that a group of Japanese students were charged £970 for a meal in Venice close to St Marks Square in 2018. In such scenarios, a judicial system is vital. It ensures market fairness by penalizing dishonest behavior, fostering trust among buyers, and stimulating economic growth through honest transactions. The Consumer

Protection law is a good example, protect consumers from fraud, misrepresentation, and other unfair business practices.

Honesty not only attracts repeat business but also helps sellers build a reputation through word-of-mouth recommendations from satisfied customers. For example, if a customer visits a barbershop with excellent service and receives a stylish haircut, they may recommend the barbershop to friends. In this way, honesty toward one customer in the market system can lead to a multiplier effect of subsequent business opportunities. Accumulating a reputation through honesty can result in significant business growth. In the 18th century, during Adam Smith's era, reputation accumulation was already vital for economic development. In today's digital age, the importance of reputation has only increased. In the past, without the internet, reputation spread mainly through word-of-mouth recommendations, broadcasting, or printed materials. Today, customer reviews and experiences are disseminated widely online, allowing businesses with good reputations to reach further and secure more opportunities. Conversely, negative reviews can result in greater business losses than before.

The Free Market Fosters Contract Integrity

In the marketplace, reputation bolsters the integrity of contracts. To safeguard their reputations, rights, and profits, both buyers and sellers are more willing to formalize their commitments in writing. For example, a seller might guarantee to ship goods upon receiving payment, while a buyer might agree to pay within three months of receiving an invoice. In a market economy, both parties are inclined to demonstrate their honesty through written agreements. Beyond showcasing honesty, another reason the market enhances contract integrity under capitalism is the role of the judiciary in upholding written agreements. When transaction details and commitments are documented, either party can seek judicial intervention in the event of a dispute. The judicial system, acting as an impartial third party, will adjudicate based on the contract's terms. However, the establishment of contract integrity requires fair justice. If the judicial system is biased, and one party has privileges that make them more likely to win disputes for unfair reasons, signing contracts in advance becomes meaningless. Thus, fair justice is a natural outcome of a market economy.

The Free Market Encourages Responsible Behavior

The free market mechanism also fosters responsible behavior among individuals and businesses regarding their societal impacts and business practices. This is primarily because profit is the market's only benchmark. When everyone can freely decide on investments and products while competing equally with others, they become very cautious about their business conduct. Since business investments are made from their own funds, they know that they risk losing their capital if they engage in market violations such as deceiving consumers. At best, their reputation will suffer, resulting in a loss of customers and future profits. At worst, violating societal norms might lead trading partners to exposure their actions, resulting legal consequences.

Self-Interest Turns into Considering Others: The Unexpected Benefits of Free Market

The market mechanism, often referred to as the invisible hand, not only promotes economic wealth accumulation but also upholds human virtues such as honest transactions, maintaining reputations, contractual integrity, and responsible behavior. People are inherently self-interested, driving them to produce for profit. As previously explained, achieving profit requires offering valuable goods or services to the market, thereby transforming self-interest into *altruistic alike behaviors.* When every market transaction involves both parties providing value and achieving win-win outcomes, these positive transactions cumulatively benefit society. The brilliance of the market mechanism lies in the fact that while individuals seek personal gain without intentionally contributing to social morality, the overall result is the establishment of societal morals and norms. These altruistic alike behaviors, result achieved by market mechanism, is the same that of true altruistic behaviors - even though people are not acting altruistically, other participants in the market receive the same benefits as if they were.

Capitalism, as a system that encourages competition and progress, is often misconstrued as one that prioritizes survival of the fittest over human morality. This view is a significant misconception and overly simplistic. While competition exists among sellers, the relationships between customers and sellers, investors and employees, and governments and citizens within a capitalist society are fundamentally cooperative. Sellers provide goods to buyers for money, workers offer labor for wages, and citizens pay taxes for public services. In essence, all parties must provide value to one another to achieve their own interests, resulting in mutually beneficial outcomes without inherent conflict.

Preconditions for Ethical Behavior in Free Markets

In societies with well-developed market economies, collaboration among strangers has become a common aspect of daily life. Whether it involves depositing life savings in a bank or purchasing a bottle of water at a convenience store, these economic activities rely on mutual trust. Without honesty and trust, the numerous transactions that drive a market economy would be unachievable. Modern civilization has created a moral and virtuous society that is unprecedented, whether these ethical behaviors stem from genuine goodwill or self-interest.

Before capitalism, human nature was generally predisposed to avoid interactions with strangers, often reacting with distrust or violence towards individuals outside their immediate family or tribe. However, modern civilization, or capitalism, has significantly altered human nature by reducing the impulse to distrust outsiders, a transformation that can rightly be described as a "cultural revolution".

However, the existence of a free market alone is insufficient to ensure the mutual confidence, commercial integrity, and behaviors of creating values for others previously mentioned. An effective punitive mechanism is essential[47]. While honesty is the only path to long-term benefits in the market, some individuals inevitably violate ethical standards for short-term gains, thus undermining the free market's effectiveness. For example, if someone intentionally defaults on a loan, banks must raise interest rates for all borrowers to manage risk, leading to higher borrowing costs and reduced loan availability, which harms both buyers and sellers. This demonstrates how a few non-compliant individuals can impose costs on the entire market. Even if nine out of ten people are honest, the fear of one dishonest person can deter transactions. Therefore, establishing an effective punitive mechanism is the best way to prevent such issues and maximize market efficiency.

A punitive mechanism, in essence, means rewarding honesty and promise-keeping while punishing rule violations. As previously discussed, while the free market encourages ethical behavior and enables those who create value through honesty to gain wealth, it cannot completely prevent dishonest or unethical conduct. To truly realize capitalism, we need public authority intervention to ensure a fair legal system. Since everyone's time and energy are limited, it is challenging to determine effectively whether a stranger or business opportunity is deceptive. The role of a fair judicial system is to ensure that dishonest and illegal actions are punished, allowing everyone in the market to engage confidently in productive activities and create mutual benefits.

Is Morality Derived from Self-Interest Hypocritical?

Some might suggest that capitalism creates a superficial harmony in society, arguing that this peace is insincere and does not reflect genuine human values. They believe the goodwill shown between people in a free market is not heartfelt but rather a result of self-interest. In contrast, a society that truly upholds humanistic ideals should see people acting kindly and benevolently out of genuine selfless intent, not self-interest. It is important to stress that in a capitalist system, individuals provide value to others primarily to pursue their own interests, not out of a desire to do good. Caring others' needs is just a secondary effect; the main intent is self-benefit. But think about this: as long as someone is willing to provide products and services that others need, does their original intention really matter?

Genuine Intentions May Not Be Important

Firstly, it is important to reiterate that human nature is inherently self-interested, a characteristic that is unchangeable. While humans are not entirely selfish, their concern for others is generally limited to those within a certain range of familiarity. It is unrealistic to expect people to care for strangers they have never met. Secondly, even with the technological advancements foreseeable in the near future, we cannot fully discern others' true intentions. Most individuals express their thoughts and emphasize their sincerity verbally, yet it is well known that everyone lies to some extent to conceal their true thoughts. We must judge people by their actions rather than their words. If Julius Caesar had foreseen Brutus's assassination, Brutus might have been eliminated beforehand, potentially altering the course of history. Thus, assessing a society's moral standards should be based on behavior rather than intentions.

For example, a farmer who grows crops and sells them at the market fulfills the food needs of many people. However, the farmer's primary motivation is not altruism, but rather earning a living. From a market economy perspective, this is perfectly acceptable. Similarly, if I visit a café and receive excellent service from a barista whose main goal is to ensure my return, rather than genuine friendship, is that really a problem? As long as the service improves my mood and I enjoy my time, the barista's true intentions are irrelevant.

Furthermore, rather than imposing or preaching people to consider others' needs, focusing on actions rather than intentions is a more effective approach to achieving moral behavior. Adam Smith noted that self-interest and the pursuit of profit are not inherently negative. Compared to using public authority to preach morality, granting people the freedom to pursue self-interest can generate greater societal benefits. This is evident in real life. Acting on providing values for others out of self-interest is not hypocritical; rather, leveraging self-interest is the best way to create a stable and sustainable moral society.

Ideally, everyone would genuinely consider others and contribute to societal well-being without the motivation of self-interest. However, since human self-interest is unchangeable, we should create a fair and free market where people provide value to others for profit. Ignoring individual self-interest and attempting to create an ideal society through moral or religious preaching is hypocritical and unsustainable. In such societies, people may speak of ethics, but their primary concern remains self-interest. For the example, the Catholic Church, before the reformation, highly valued ethics, yet it sold indulgences, a hypocritical practice that ultimately led to the Reformation.

Capitalism as the primary system: Virtue as a Complement

It is not wrong promoting and educating people about humanistic virtues and considering others in modern society at all. Upholding concepts like freedom, equality, and democracy is undoubtedly beneficial. A modern society that realizes humanistic values must also emphasize the teaching of virtues and altruistic behavior. My argument has two key points. First, I must acknowledge that achieving humanistic values requires more than just a free market. Marx's criticisms of capitalism are not entirely baseless; market economies do have imperfections. Even with a fair judicial system and a generally benevolent society, we cannot completely eliminate dishonest merchants and rule-breakers. Therefore, promoting moral virtues and altruism is crucial for enhancing modern society.

Second, the market itself is fragile. Establishing a market system takes time, but destroying it can be easy. Earlier, we discussed how the free market fosters people to consider others' needs and creates value, which are based on long-term interests. The market's strength lies in motivating people to consistently practice honesty to build their reputations and long-term profits. Unfortunately, not everyone in the market understands this principle. Some individuals are short-sighted, focused only on immediate gains, and therefore they might choose to break market rules. Although such behavior is punishable and unsustainable in a healthy capitalist system, we must ensure that those willing to risk long-term benefits for short-term gains remain a minority. Otherwise, the example set by unscrupulous merchants could lead to more rule-breakers, weakening the market system.

Protecting the market requires not only enhancing the judiciary and ensuring fairness and freedom but also promoting education about the market system and long-term benefits. We must inform society that adhering to market rules and achieving long-term benefits outweighs the short-term gains of dishonest actions. Conveying that keep creating values for others over long term equates to self-interest will ensure the stability and prosperity of the market economy.

However, while both the market economy and virtue promotion contribute to realizing humanistic values, their importance and sequence differ. How should modern society balance these elements to achieve these values? Relying solely on changing human thoughts and nature to achieve social benefits is unrealistic. Therefore, I advocate prioritizing a market economy that encourages self-interest, with the promotion of altruistic virtues as a secondary measure. Although changing people's mindset through moral education may not be highly efficient, it is not entirely ineffective. For example, martyrs and missionaries who died for their Christian faith. However, such examples were exceptions, not the norm.

A society that only promotes altruism without encouraging self-interest through a market mechanism is fundamentally flawed and cannot be considered modern. Only within a capitalist system, where citizens can achieve personal happiness and create societal welfare in a free market, can the majority voluntarily create value for others. Adding humanistic value promotion and education onto this foundation forms a well-functioning system for modern society. In a capitalist system, humanistic virtues and self-interest are not mutually exclusive but can coexist and be realized simultaneously.

3. Capitalism and Freedom

If one were to summarize the key characteristic of the capitalist system with a single word, "freedom" would be the most appropriate term. More accurately, the capitalist free market system permits individuals to make choices freely and obliges them to take responsibility for their choices. Friedrich Hayek, a prominent 20th-century economist, famously remarked that the most ideal societal state is one filled with freedom.

The definition of freedom varies widely. Simply put, a person who is free can make choices based on their own will without fear of threats or harm from others. Undoubtedly, the ideal situation for an individual is to choose their lifestyle according to their needs and desires. In contrast, the concept opposing freedom is slavery. In other words, an enslaved person cannot pursue their desired life and actions according to their wishes. Their fate is controlled by others, preventing them from making their own decisions. Of course, these definitions of freedom and slavery are extreme. In today's society, it is rare to find someone who is entirely enslaved and unable to decide anything for themselves. Likewise, no one has complete freedom to do whatever they wish. In modern society, absolute enslavement is virtually nonexistent, but those who earn an income are required to pay taxes, and no one is free to refuse this obligation.

Capitalism and Individual Freedom

The brilliance of the capitalist system is in its respect for individual freedom of choice and action, allowing everyone to pursue wealth and happiness based on their own judgment, while establishing orderly and humane social norms at the same time. The approach to creating economic operational standards differs significantly between the free market and a planned economy. Those in favor of socialist planned economy believe that letting the market develop freely would result in chaos. Thus, central government or public authorities need to regulate the economy to set operational rules, aiming to minimize social problems like the wealth gap. Conversely, the logic of the capitalist system is that economic operational standards naturally develop. When everyone in the economy produces based on their judgment and creates value for others, everyone's desires will be met. Moreover, since the nature of trade is mutually beneficial, individuals and businesses in the market understand that honesty is the key to maximizing benefits, maintaining social norms.

A planned economy seeks to control every aspect of economic activity through central regulation, essentially trying to change human nature by having public authority decide what should be produced. The market economy, on the other hand, does not attempt to change human nature; it uses human characteristics to drive social and economic progress. In capitalism, individuals are not required to practice self-denial; they can freely choose to take investment risks when opportunities arise. Capitalism also does not force people to save; they can consume and invest as they see fit. In other words, we can pursue happiness in our own way. The core of the capitalist economy is to provide incentives for individuals to do good, rather than through administrative or legal coercion. The market economy shows that written administrative orders are not the only way to achieve human morality. We just need a good system that allows people to benefit from creating value for others, leading society toward harmony. This approach is much more cost-effective than enforcing administrative orders, and it allows people to enjoy unrestricted freedom, achieving mutual benefits.

Granting Freedom to Individuals Is Crucial

Individual freedom is crucial for the development of an economy. Individual freedom contributes to wealth creation in two primary ways. First, individuals within an economy are more familiar with their immediate environments than a central government is. For example, the locals are the best judges of whether a food stall or a café should be established in a night market, or whether a café or a bar should open in a bustling city center, not detached policymakers. It is more effective to delegate decision-making power to the populace, allowing them the freedom to make more accurate judgments regarding economic development. Second, granting individuals freedom enhances economic efficiency. When an entrepreneur or a company identifies a business opportunity, they can act faster than a large, bureaucratic government. They can also resolve issues more swiftly. Because individuals and businesses are smaller in scale, they are less likely to be hindered by bureaucracy and slow responses, unlike the government.

Beyond benefiting material economic development, granting freedom to society also has positive effects on individual morality. I will outline two points here. First, the existence of a capitalist system encourages responsible behavior within society. In capitalism, everyone can produce and trade freely within the legal framework. Therefore, the market collectively determines the availability of goods, trends, and prices, which are crucial for entrepreneurs, investors, and workers. In other words, no single individual can control or predict market trends.

Every individual's actions in the market are driven by self-interest, but since no one can control the market, the only option is to work diligently on what they can manage independently, which is to honestly create the best products and services to provide value to others. I term this *responsible behavior*. If sellers fail to create value, they may incur losses and must bear the consequences. The market mechanism promotes this responsible behavior because entrepreneurs invest their own money, unlike following orders in state-owned enterprises or volunteering in charitable organizations. Mistakes or laziness can lead to significant financial losses, not just embarrassment. If consumers are dissatisfied with a seller's incompetence or errors, it can damage the seller's reputation and result in financial ruin. The market acts as a punitive mechanism, penalizing those who harm the market through reduced sales or losses. Thus, creating value for others and hoping for profit in return, driven by responsible behavior, is the only way to survive in the market.

Second, free competition is a fundamental aspect of capitalism, driving progress for individuals and society alike. In the market, many strive to achieve profit and returns through hard work. Given the limited nature of market resources and demand, this pursuit of profit naturally leads to competition. Capitalism's emphasis on a free market allows anyone with a viable idea to enter, invest, and produce. As a result, those offering similar products or services inevitably compete.

While competition may not be enjoyable for the competitors and carries the risk of failure, it benefits society by fostering innovation and progress. Market forces determine product quality, and to outcompete others, one must produce superior products or enhance efficiency to reduce costs and prices. This innovation and progress are the fruits of free competition. This drive for progress has led to unprecedented wealth over the past few centuries, while elevating cooperation and honesty within society. Weiying Zhang of Peking University suggests that the driving force behind human progress is not merely technological advancements but the advent of modern capitalism and the free market system, which spur innovation, enabling modern civilization to progress. For instance, ancient China experienced numerous technological innovations but remained a small-scale agrarian economy until the late Qing dynasty due to the absence of a modern market economy. Even in the 21st century, mainland China struggles to be seen as a society that fully respects humanistic values, likely due to the lack of a developed market economy.

Some claim that free competition opposes humanistic values, arguing that a humanistic society should be harmonious and cooperative. Indeed, no one naturally enjoys competition. Yet competition mainly occurs among producers of similar goods, not between labor and capital or within supply chains. An entrepreneur's transactions with customers and upstream sellers involve mutual exchanges of money for goods or services, which is inherently a win-win situation. Even the labor-capital relationship, criticized by Marx, involves the exchange of labor for wages. Competition primarily occurs horizontally or within industries.

What's more, while free competition is a reality, it is not a life-and-death struggle. Competition is necessary to assess whether products and services meet market demands. If someone loses in competition, they can switch industries or offer different products or services. Competition has always been a norm in human societies, even before capitalism. Therefore, we should not exaggerate market competition. Instead of eliminating free competition, we should aim to regulate it to ensure fair competition, prohibiting cheating, malicious competition, and unethical practices. To foster such a competitive environment, public authorities must design and enforce fair and effective judicial systems to penalize rule-breakers. Additionally, through education, we must teach people to respect market rules and to produce and provide value honestly, making it clear that this is the only way to succeed in market competition.

The Role of Public Authority in a Free Market

I want to emphasize that while I continually highlight the importance of freedom within the capitalist system in this chapter, I do not advocate for anarchism. Anarchism argues that government influence on the market should be rejected, and that allowing the market to operate autonomously is the best way to develop the economy. It sees government intervention as a hindrance to market development. While modern economics often supports government intervention—such as the adjustment of interest rates to stimulate the economy, or the increase of government spending to boost employment—to maintain socio-economic stability, these interventions can be counterproductive and may have significant economic side effects. Nevertheless, the idea of having "zero government role" in the market is, in my view, overly extreme. Freedom alone cannot develop a modern capitalist system; the protection and support of public authority are crucial too.

The success of the capitalist system over the past 300 years is closely tied to the role of public authority. The primary function of government is to reduce transaction costs[48] within the market, making commerce more efficient. Historically, people have traded freely without much government restriction, yet advanced commercial capitalism did not develop until the 18th century. This indicates that laissez-faire policies alone are not enough to develop capitalism. As previously stated, the core of a market economy is that individuals can engage in economic activities freely and equally, without restrictions or class distinctions. However, these elements alone are insufficient; a thriving market and economy require the presence of public authority.

In the market, some level of distrust is inevitable. There will be disputes between buyers and sellers, or cases in which one party fails to honor their commitments. Some public authority's intervention is needed in such situations to resolve disputes through a fair judicial system, ensuring that all market participants can trade without fear of deceit. Market logic often relies on repeated transactions, where dishonest behavior by merchants can be punished by consumers choosing not to buy from them in the future or spreading negative reviews.

However, some market transactions are one-time deals. In such cases, sellers do not need to worry about their dishonesty affecting their reputation, so they can freely harm buyers. A prime example of this is financial institutions: when bank customers deposit money for savings or investment, the funds are singular. If the bank misbehaves or collapses, customers bear substantial costs and losses, making it difficult for them to protect themselves through market mechanisms. Here, the government's role is crucial. The government must oversee banks and financial institutions, allowing only well-managed and compliant entities to operate, ensuring the market functions properly. The same applies to higher education; young people only have one chance to attend university. A wrong choice may result in significant costs. Therefore, government oversight of higher education, including the establishment of public universities to ensure quality education, helps stabilize the market and cultivate talent.

Additionally, public authority can influence economic behavior by providing incentives. For example, if a city suffers from pollution due to excessive vehicle traffic, the government can impose an entry tax on external vehicles or provide subsidies for low-emission vehicles to address environmental issues. I do not support the use of strict measures, such as banning certain vehicles from city centers or prohibiting the sale of environmentally harmful products. In economics, offering incentives to solve problems is often more cost-effective and less coercive than rigid administrative policies. Just as people strive for profit, they will also respond to incentives. Allowing all choices to remain available while using incentives to change the attractiveness of different options benefits both market freedom and development.

If we liken the operation of the economy to an exciting football match, then the government should is the referee, not a player. The referee's role is to ensure fair play, not to determine the events of the game, which depend on the players' performance. Players, as professionals, must freely exercise their skills to win the game.

Understanding the impact of public authority on market development requires examining how planned economies work. In any economic system, there are individuals with different ideas, needs, and preferences. Some prefer to work harder for greater rewards, others prefer more leisure, some have strong business acumen and take investment risks, while others are risk-averse and prefer a stable salary. In a planned economy, such personal choices do not exist. The government dictates production, consumption, and pricing. This model is bound to fail. Firstly, the government, as a minority in terms of number of people, cannot fully understand the diverse needs of all individuals. If public authority monopolizes production decisions, many needs will remain unmet, leading to dissatisfaction among citizens. Secondly, according to public economic policy theory, policymakers act less cautiously when they do not bear the full consequences of their decisions. If they do not have to pay for their mistakes, unlike entrepreneurs in free markets who may face a loss or even bankruptcy when business fails, if there is no skin in the game, why should they care? Delegating decision-making to the market increases the chances of producing desired goods and services.

Moreover, the significant power of the judiciary makes the government prone to abuse. Government officials, being human, are susceptible to greed, and they may skew economic decisions in their favor, leading to rule of man. Therefore, limiting government power is crucial to preventing authoritarianism and protecting individual freedoms.

Capitalism and Democracy

Arguably the two most influential economists of the 20th century are John Maynard Keynes and Friedrich August Hayek. Both were staunch supporters of market economies and critics of planned economies, yet their perspectives on how capitalist economies should operate were vastly different.

Hayek believed that government should not interfere in the market, whereas Keynes argued that markets sometimes fail and government intervention can make market self-regulation more efficient. Hayek viewed economic cycles as inevitable in a free market, and that central bank intervention hinders recovery, while Keynes saw economic downturns as a result of insufficient demand, requiring government action to revive the economy. Hayek stressed the critical role of the price mechanism in resource allocation and self-regulation within the free market, discouraging intervention, whereas Keynes believed that market mechanisms often fail, and that government spending is necessary to boost the economy.

Their opposing views led to decades-long debates throughout the 20th century. Even today, there is no consensus among scholars on the proper role of public authority in capitalism and free markets.

Keynes and Hayek as Supporters of Democracy

While Keynes and Hayek fiercely debated government intervention in markets, surprisingly, they shared a unified stance on democracy.[49] Both economists emphasized that the economic system's vitality lies in protecting Western democratic institutions. Their views were significantly influenced by the historical period they lived through, from the tumultuous 1920s to the post-World War II era in the 1950s. This era was marked by global economic crises, the ascendance of Nazi militarism, and the Second World War, all of which profoundly shaped Keynes's and Hayek's economic and political philosophies.

Democratic elections, characterized by universal suffrage and equal representation, embody democracy's fundamental protection of individual rights. In contrast to authoritarian regimes, democracy decentralizes power and safeguards human rights. It allows individuals to participate in their own governance through voting and political activism, thereby checking governmental authority. Crucially, democracy fosters stability; transitions of power are typically peaceful, contrasting sharply with the instability seen in autocratic regimes. Moreover, democratic countries tend to avoid interstate conflicts, contributing to global peace.[50]

Keynes vehemently opposed Nazism and totalitarianism, though today this is a universally accepted stance. In Keynes's view, the rise of Nazism in Germany was closely linked to the economic crises of the 1930s and the erroneous economic policies of the Weimar government.[51] The Wall Street Crash of 1929 had repercussions across Europe during the 1930s, leading to the Great Depression, which was experienced around the world. However, because a significant portion of their government revenues had been allocated to World War I reparations as part of the armistice terms, Germany lacked the financial resources to stabilize its economy.

Consequently, as Germany faced economic crises and fiscal pressures, confidence eroded. The rapid depreciation of the German mark resulted in severe hyperinflation, causing essential goods prices to skyrocket and rapidly diminishing the purchasing power of the middle class, pushing many into poverty. This explains why there was considerable public support for Nazism in the 1930s, according to Keynes. He viewed the incompetence of the Weimar German government's economic policies as complicit in this tragedy. Keynes argued that despite substantial fiscal pressures, the German government had the capability to implement relief policies to alleviate the situation.

On the contrary, Keynes viewed the US government's crisis management approach as considerably more sensible. Following the stock market crash, President Franklin D. Roosevelt implemented the

New Deal, [52] actively intervening to boost market recovery, stimulate consumption and investment, create jobs, and reform the financial system. This proactive stance enabled the United States to emerge from the crisis in a short time and prevented the emergence of totalitarianism within its borders. According to Keynes, this governmental intervention underpinned the United States' social and political stability, effectively safeguarding the democratic framework. Therefore, Keynes argued that the issue was less about whether governmental market intervention was necessary, but rather that the ethical conduct, principles, and self-discipline of political leaders was. Keynes acknowledged that governmental intervention symbolized an exercise of authority, yet he contended that as long as public officials maintained ethical standards and recognized that economic progress predominantly hinges on market dynamics, governmental intervention would serve as a supplementary, rather than overriding, force. It is imperative for policymakers to discern the boundaries of intervention and refrain from crossing them to ensure the safety of governmental intervention and safeguard democratic institutions. Furthermore, according to Keynes, redistributive efforts undertaken through governmental intervention establish a minimum standard of living, thereby contributing to the stability of democratic governance.

Hayek did not question Keynes's intention to protect democracy, nor did he dispute that Keynes's advocacy for intervention was meant to uphold democratic values. Hayek strongly disagreed, however, with Keynes's reliance on the morality of policymakers as a basis for government intervention in the market. Hayek was more skeptical of human nature and believed that societal welfare should not depend on individual morality and goodwill. Instead, he argued for the establishment of institutions to regulate human behavior. Hayek maintained that government officials, being human, are inherently self-interested. When the government intervenes in the market and makes decisions with incomplete information, officials are likely to adjust policies to benefit their political or financial interests.

Government intervention signifies an expansion of power, akin to opening Pandora's box—once it begins, it is challenging to rein in. Hayek believed that excessive economic intervention could lead to socialism or a planned economy, ultimately culminating in fascism, regardless of how good the initial intentions might be. In today's society, he argued, we should strive to balance private and public power, rather than to transfer power to the government and expect public officials to act ethically.

Although both scholars passed away before the 21st century, their debates remain relevant and continue to be discussed today. Regardless of their differences, both agreed that economic freedom is fundamental to personal liberty; without economic freedom, individual and political freedoms cannot endure.

Capitalism As Foundation of Democracy

Milton Friedman, a prominent economist, provided a comprehensive explanation of the link between capitalism and democracy. In his book *Capitalism and Freedom,* [53] Friedman posits that economic freedom is essential for political freedom. He suggests that a democratic system cannot thrive without capitalism because capitalism separates economic rights from governmental political power. This separation allows individuals to freely pursue wealth and simultaneously seek political influence to protect their property. Thus, capitalism inherently decentralizes public power, balancing power and allowing economic and political rights to check each other.

At the heart of capitalism is respect for private property, a value that aligns with democracy's respect for individual rights. Historical events such as the Magna Carta and the French Revolution, which were pivotal in the decentralization of power, were initially driven by the bourgeoisie's fight for property rights. Capitalism advocates for decentralization, ensuring that key economic decisions are made by market participants. Furthermore, a capitalist system motivates individuals to exercise their rights and monitor the government to protect their property. These examples demonstrate that capitalism and democracy share many fundamental principles. The market economy provides individuals with the means to sustain capitalism, thereby indirectly supporting the democratic system.

Capitalism serves as a foundational prerequisite for a democratic system. Historically, no country has achieved a true democratic society without first establishing a capitalist framework. Middle Eastern and West Asian countries such as Iraq, Afghanistan, and Tunisia have attempted to introduce democratic systems under various circumstances, only to result in disorder and an inability to establish social order. This failure can be primarily attributed to the absence of capitalist traditions, such as private property rights and the rule of law. Consequently, imposing a democratic system in these countries was bound to fail.

To realize democracy, citizens must deeply understand their rights, such as private property, the costs associated with freedom, and their corresponding responsibilities. These traditions are typically developed through the experience of a capitalist market economy and cannot be established overnight. Implementing democracy in societies without a tradition of economic freedom can lead to citizens neglecting their freedoms and rights, resulting in severe government corruption. Or citizens may rely on the benefits of democracy without accepting their responsibilities, ultimately leading to the collapse of the democratic system.

The failure of the Arab Spring in 2010 is a good example. The Arab Spring was a wave of protests and revolutions that swept through the Arab world from late 2010 to early 2012, initially raising hopes for democratic reforms. However, it ultimately failed to bring true democracy to the region, leading instead to chaos, civil wars, and the restoration of authoritarian regimes in many cases. One of reasons is absence of strong middle class, which were trained to understand that democracy does not mean doing whatever one wants. As a citizen, democracy also comes with rights and responsibilities, in order to make democracy function. Politics might be abstract and difficult for people to understand, protecting property rights is more straightforward. But the concept of property rights requires a tradition of free market which is unfortunately in the Arab world.

It is essential to recognize that while capitalism is a necessary condition for democracy, it does not automatically lead to its establishment. Hong Kong illustrates this point. Since becoming a British colony in 1840, Hong Kong has never practiced genuine, one-person-one-vote elections. Despite the political conflicts between Britain and China, Hong Kong has developed into a world-class financial center. From the 19th century onwards, Hong Kong gradually established a mature capitalist system, which included economic freedom and a fair rule of law. Similarly, Mainland China demonstrates the lack of synchronization between political freedom and economic freedom. Following its economic reforms and opening to international trade, China transitioned from a command economy to a free market. Many anticipated that democracy would emerge alongside economic freedom, but this has not transpired in the 21st century. Likewise, pre-World War II Nazi Germany, Fascist Italy and Spain, and militaristic Japan embraced capitalism economically but had no political alignment with democracy.

Thus, capitalism does not necessarily lead to democracy, but it is a prerequisite. Without a free market, democracy is unlikely to succeed.

Capitalism and Consumerism?

There is no doubt that capitalism, as the dominant economic system of human civilization, has brought about unprecedented material prosperity. In modern society, many people question whether this material wealth has genuinely resulted in spiritual well-being. Worker exploitation, rampant consumerism among white-collar workers, and the housing affordability crisis in big cities will be familiar phenomena to many readers. These issues suggest that the development of capitalism and the explosion of material wealth have not necessarily improved human life.

Even as a supporter of the free market, I have also questioned the correlation between the capitalist system and human happiness. For example, in 2020, the global per capita GDP was approximately $10, 000, whereas in 1980, it was only $2, 500 (Current US$).[54] In other words, over these 40 years, the average person earned four times more money, or we had four times more material goods. But the question remains: has our happiness increased fourfold along with our income? The answer from the philosopher Herbert Marcus would be a no.

Is Capitalism a Form of Comfortable Authoritarianism?

Many people believe that capitalism is essentially about consumerism and that endless consumption can make people morally corrupt. One of the most outspoken critics of capitalism is Herbert Marcuse. Marcuse was a Jewish man who fled Nazi Germany to escape persecution and found freedom in America. Despite enjoying this freedom, he was a harsh critic of America's capitalist system. An open Marxist, Marcuse called America's advanced industrial society a form of "non-terroristic authoritarianism" or "repressive tolerance". These terms might sound contradictory, but Marcuse thought they fit together under capitalism.[55]

Marcuse believed that capitalism gives people a comfortable, materially rich life, but one that is not actually free. People might seem to live well and make their own choices, but they are controlled by the system and gradually lose their freedom without noticing. This comfort hides the authoritarian nature of capitalism. Marcuse pointed out two main features of capitalist control: it avoids violence , so it does not seem scary. Plus, capitalism is good at placating those who oppose the system, which in turn peacefully maintains the system. By constantly providing material goods, capitalism keeps people wanting more, making them willingly work and stay under its control and to serve their own desires.

Marcuse posits that many of the demands spawned by modern capitalism, which he terms *False Needs*, are superfluous. The artificiality of these needs stems from our capacity to find value and contentment without succumbing to extravagant consumption. Examples such as Wagyu beef over regular beef, smartphones versus basic models, and designer handbags rather than street vendor alternatives fall under the category of "False Needs". Marcuse argues that our perceptions of necessity, taste, and aesthetics are often shaped not by personal choice but by the pervasive consumerist ethos of society. Capitalism instills in us attitudes, habits, and desires oriented toward luxury that, once embraced, become difficult to relinquish, as encapsulated in the adage, "easier to go from frugality to luxury than vice versa". This consumerist ethos, he asserts, does not equate to true freedom but rather ensnares us in a perpetual cycle of consumption that superficially fulfills our desires while leading us into a bottomless pit of need.

Marcuse's criticism of the current state of capitalism is not unfounded. I agree that the advancement of capitalism does not necessarily equate to increased happiness, and that the prevalence of consumerism and impulse buying in contemporary society is undeniable. I question whether it is entirely fair, however, to place all responsibility for these issues on the capitalist system.

It is important to recognize that capitalism and market economies have expanded our choices, allowing us the freedom to pursue our aspirations—including seeking happiness and fulfilling our sense of purpose, even if it involves satisfying superficial desires. My point of emphasis lies in the definition of freedom, which is complex and nuanced. It does not merely entail unrestricted self-indulgence free from oppression or coercion; rather, true freedom involves making informed choices, weighing the consequences of each option carefully, and assuming accountability for those decisions. Capitalism, in the context of human history, stands as the system offering the greatest array of choices, empowering individuals to choose and shoulder corresponding responsibilities.

Freedom Means More Choices

In considering human freedom of choice and its associated responsibilities, I find Jean-Paul Sartre's insights particularly compelling. Interestingly, both Sartre and Marcuse self-identify as Marxists, yet Sartre's perspective on freedom can be seen as a counterpoint to Marcuse's critique of capitalism. Sartre posits that in a free society, along with freedom comes not only responsibility but also a profound burden for individuals. He argues that humans are not born with inherent meaning in this world; our existence may be arbitrary, with life spanning several decades before eventual death.

In pre-modern Western societies, Catholicism prescribed moral conduct and good deeds as pathways to heavenly reward. In ancient China, men were expected to embody moral virtue to achieve historical renown, while women adhered to strict codes of conduct to honor their families. These cultural frameworks provided individuals with a sense of purpose and meaning. However, contemporary society increasingly challenges these traditional notions of life's purpose, often viewed as outdated or irrelevant. Modern society, in contrast, lacks authoritative guidance on life's meaning and purpose, leaving individuals to seek answers independently. One can prioritize romantic love as the center of life, or in turn elevate family, career, hobbies, or academic pursuits—all within legal and ethical boundaries. Sartre argues that maximizing choice epitomizes freedom; hence, capitalism, by offering a wide range of life choices, enables individuals to pursue their existential goals freely.

If capitalism is considered unfree, then we must consider societies and nations without capitalism as point of comparison. In the former Soviet Union and communist China, spiritually, individuals' values had to align with state authority; the government defined right and wrong for the masses, leaving no room for individuals to define their own meaning. Moreover, materially, due to the lack of market incentives, these societies often faced shortages, and even struggled to provide sufficient food. Criticizing the false needs within affluent capitalism might thus seem excessively stringent when compared to the alternatives.

From Sartre, since life lacks inherent meaning, we navigate our life guided by personal ideas and the future remains uncertain. In capitalist societies, where we have more choices and can select what suits us best from numerous options, is not this a manifestation of freedom? Certainly, some may find fulfillment and realize their values through their choices, while others may succumb to insatiable desires, unable to extricate themselves from their depths. Individuals must carefully consider their needs and take responsibility for the consequences of their choices, without blaming others or societal environments such as the capitalist system. While some achieve value, others may choose to indulge in desires and fall into moral decay, but is that the fault of the capitalist system, or of the individual?

Certainly, I acknowledge that a significant portion of society may succumb to self-indulgence due to consumerism. However, capitalism's provision of an abundance of choices is not the instigator, but rather individuals' lack of awareness of the consequences of their choices, or their refusal to take responsibility for them. Achieving this awareness necessitates the importance of disciplines like philosophy and humanities. Only when individuals grasp the true meaning of freedom can they avoid falling into the trap of unchecked desires.

Consumerism in capitalist societies is just superficial. In free markets, beyond consumption, there exist numerous opportunities for individuals to realize their life's values. The essence of freedom lies in choice, and when capitalism provides everyone with more options and possibilities, criticizing the system for offering too many choices seems both disingenuous and a refusal to take responsibility for one's own decisions.

Let us return to the initial concern about the explosion of wealth brought about by capitalism and whether or not it necessarily leads to corresponding happiness. As modern society advances, people may face additional challenges, but they also gain the potential to earn more money and achieve their life goals and purposes. In a developed capitalist system, individuals can choose to work harder for financial gain or opt for a simpler, less stressful lifestyle, thus expanding their options for how to live. Furthermore, holding capitalism responsible when individuals fall into excessive desires seems unfair. While capitalism offers more choices, achieving true freedom requires personal self-discipline and the courage to take responsibility. Freedom does not inherently lead to happiness; it only guarantees the ability to choose what one wants. Ultimately, the outcomes of these choices must be shouldered by those who make them.

4. Capitalism and Social Equality

Since the onset of the 21st century, the term "capitalism" appears to be acquiring increasingly negative connotations, both in the West and the East. A 2019 survey among young Americans indicated that nearly 50% held a negative view of capitalism, with this sentiment showing a yearly increase. This trend in the United States, the world's most advanced capitalist nation, is particularly worrisome.[56]

From the critiques of Marx in the 19th century to those in the 21st century, capitalism has consistently faced criticism. Key points include the excessive concentration of capital, corporate monopolies, and the exploitation of workers. In essence, all these criticisms point to the inherent inequality within the capitalist system.

The Lower Class of Society Benefits More from Capitalism

The assertion that modern capitalism widens the wealth gap appears overly critical to me. Upon examining the historical development of human societies, the notion that capitalism inherently leads to polarization does not hold up. Firstly, it is indisputable that modern capitalism has brought material prosperity to society as a whole. Additionally, throughout most of history, every individual benefits from the presence of a free market: people experience improved living standards, even more so in the lower strata of society than the upper strata.

Earlier, we discussed how the driving forces behind economic and social advancement in a capitalist system are the pursuit of wealth and technological progress spurred by competition. Consider the example of airline tickets.[57] In the 1960s, flying was an expensive luxury. For example, a round-trip flight from London to New York could cost about $550 back then, which is equivalent to $4, 000 in today's currency. It is no exaggeration to say that flight prices have become 3-5 times higher.

Aside from technical factors like more fuel-efficient aircrafts or improved airline management efficiency, a major factor in cheaper tickets was the U.S. government's deregulation of the airline industry in the 1970s, which ended the monopoly of a few major airlines. Increased competition led to lower ticket prices, and consumers were the primary beneficiaries of this marketization.

Nevertheless, the significance of reduced ticket prices differs greatly between the wealthy and the poor. For the wealthy, cheaper tickets due to competition might mean a few more vacations a year or the ability to travel further afield. Even without price reductions, the wealthy could still afford to pay for necessary travel. For the poor, however, a substantial reduction in ticket prices could make the difference between unaffordable travel and newfound possibility. In other words, the price drop is a luxury for the rich but a new opportunity for the common people. The greatest beneficiaries of the wealth and progress brought by a capitalist market economy are often not the upper class but the general populace.[58]

The free market simultaneously asserts that equal opportunity is essential for economic development. Classical market theory posits that only when everyone has equal opportunities to engage in production, trade, and consumption can the work motivation and potential of each market participant be fully realized. Regardless of one's identity, as long as they have a viable idea and the capacity to produce or provide services, they can enter the market and compete with other businesses. The market does not allow any privileged class to monopolize industries and exclude others. In a capitalist market, survival hinges on the ability to provide the best products and services at the most competitive prices, gaining customer recognition and orders. This principle applies universally, irrespective of class, background, skin color, or race. In a capitalist system, a doctor's ability to practice depends on their medical skills and reputation, not their social class. Similarly, a restaurant's success depends on the quality of its food and service, not the race or skin color of its owner. As long as individuals have the capability and competitiveness, anyone can achieve profitability in the market.

Greater Opportunities for Social Mobility Under Capitalism

Readers might be familiar with the phrase, "capitalist society is a system driven by money". This phrase may sound negative, suggesting social inequality and the undue influence of wealth. However, let us consider this issue from a different angle: is not an emphasis on money also a reflection of social equality? In Western society before the 18th century, aristocratic culture and privileges were widespread. Luxuries, real estate, and even higher education were exclusive privileges of the upper class, inaccessible to the lower classes regardless of their wealth. Similarly, many former colonial countries had racial segregation policies before gaining independence. Colonizers often had exclusive access to social resources, while the colonized frequently lacked the opportunity to pursue higher education. However, with the development of capitalism, today, anyone who can generate wealth in the market can access these resources.

Traditional Chinese society exhibited similar dynamics. You might know the social hierarchy of scholars, farmers, artisans, and merchants. Although merchants often had more money than workers and farmers, their social status was the lowest. They were required to wear specific colors and faced restrictions on land ownership. No matter how much wealth merchants accumulated through commerce, they could not surpass the social status of scholars, farmers, and artisans. Thus, the rise of modern capitalism has positively impacted social mobility. In a competitive market, individuals who can generate profits gain access to the upper levels of society. Those without money can achieve upward mobility through their intelligence and effort, despite their unchangeable birth and race.

The Chinese Economic Reform Brought About Social Mobility

The economic reform of Mainland China is a prime historical example of increased social mobility. After the Cultural Revolution ended in the 1970s, the Chinese government gradually shifted its economic policies. Transitioning from a strictly planned economy that denied private property rights, China incrementally incorporated more market elements into its economy, despite the government never officially acknowledging the adoption of a capitalist market economy. The marketization of China's economy led to a significant increase in wealth and provided opportunities for lower-class citizens to climb the social ladder and attain social status.

My mother, who was born and raised in Mainland China, experienced the Cultural Revolution and the policy of sending urban youth to rural areas. She often told me that during the later stages of the Cultural Revolution, the *"Sent-Down youth"*[59] who had been sent to the countryside were eager to return to the cities. However, returning to the cities was not a straightforward process; it occurred in slow, gradual waves. Those fortunate enough to have family connections or ties to the Communist Party could return sooner, but those without such connections had to cultivate good relationships with local rural officials, who had the power to decide when a youth could leave. Such scenarios, where public authority could determine one's fate, became rare after China initiated its reform and economic opening.

In post-reform China, the significance of being a civil servant or holding public authority diminished compared to the Cultural Revolution era. Some people argue that economic reform has resulted in inequality; however, I do not entirely agree. While disparities of income and material wealth exist, there is less fundamental inequality. Starvation due to poverty has become rare since the reform and opening, and few people's fates are entirely controlled by public authority. Compared to the planned economy of the Cultural Revolution, the Chinese economic reform has led to progress in terms of equality between civil society and public authority.

Social mobility in China did not cease with the reform; it has continued ever since. For instance, Jack Ma, who was once an English teacher in the early 1990s, became China's richest man through his own hard work and ingenuity. The Chinese government seems to recognize that economic development requires fair competition among all individuals, which stimulates the desire and talent for wealth creation. Policies such as opening the college entrance examination to provide equal educational opportunities, and allowing private enterprises to compete with state-owned enterprises, have given those without public authority the chance to attain wealth and social mobility. In a free market, key market information like prices and regulations is relatively transparent and observable by everyone. Individuals can engage in trade, collaboration, and competition. Regardless of who you are or your background, the market treats everyone equally. If you have the ability to provide value, you can earn corresponding profits and wealth.

A Planned Economy Is More Unequal

The planned economy, involves the centralized decision-making by a select group of societal elites who dictate production, pricing, distribution channels, and other economic activities through mandates. While I acknowledge the good intentions behind this elite-driven approach society should not entrust individuals with unrestricted autonomy but rather delegate economic design to the upper echelons. While I understand the initial aspirations of these planners, the practical execution often turns the purportedly egalitarian command economy into an inequitable system. Within the command economy framework, elites wield authority over economic operations, creating a disparity between them and ordinary citizens lacking such privilege. Moreover, governmental directives supersede free-market competition and price mechanisms, undermining the ability to evaluate the quality of goods and services.

Competition and pricing, essential market signals, [60] indicate the viability of enterprises and the attractiveness of products or services. Thus, higher prices may signal scarcity or superior quality, guiding market participants in investment decisions and production strategies. When government monopolizes market decision-making and essential signals are absent, economic operations become dependent on individuals with political authority. Essentially, this results in a governance-by-individuals approach. The primary challenge with governance by individuals is the inability of so-called economic elites to obtain accurate market information in the absence of demand-driven prices and other signals.

Firstly, government decisions under such conditions rely on speculation. Secondly, individuals wielding political power often make allocation judgments based on personal interests, contributing to widespread corruption and mismanagement, evident in the histories of the Soviet Union and Communist China. I posit that due to the uncontrollability of the market, market mechanisms serve as an objective and equitable allocation system. Conversely, governance by individuals relies on subjective judgments that are inevitably biased, particularly once individuals acquire power and become motivated to maintain that power, thus undermining impartiality and fairness.

Marx's Theory of Exploitation and Nozick's Criticisms

Let us delve into Marx's critique of capitalism regarding the exploitation of labor. Marx's primary critique of the free market revolves around his theory of exploitation. In his seminal work *Das Kapital,* Marx elaborates on how capitalists exploit laborers. Marx identifies two key points: firstly, he argues that the value of all goods is derived from labor, implying that this value should rightfully belong entirely to the laborers. Yet in practice, capitalists do not compensate laborers adequately relative to their contributions. Marx terms the disparity between the price of goods and the actual wages paid to laborers as surplus value. He contends that this surplus value, which should rightfully belong to laborers, is largely appropriated by capitalists, resulting in the exploitation of labor.

Secondly, Marx perceives this exploitation as a form of coerced labor because laborers lack ownership of essential production assets such as tools and machinery, which are monopolized by capitalists. Without access to these *means of production*, laborers are unable to create the value of goods and thus are compelled to accept exploitation.

Nozick's Criticism of the Exploitation Theory

Marx's theories enjoyed significant popularity until the first half of the 20th century, despite persistent criticism. However, the economic failures of communist states such as the Soviet Union, China, and Cuba led to a decline in Marx's influence. Among the critics of communism and Marx's exploitation theory, Robert Nozick stands out prominently. Nozick rejects Marx's notion of exploitation, arguing that it does not hold in a free market. He contends that due to individual differences and varying skills, the value of labor naturally varies in the labor market. Some individuals possess strong marketable skills while others possessive different skills or less valuable ones, and when they freely choose their occupations, they naturally earn different salaries.

Workers have the liberty to accept or decline job offers, and when a less-skilled worker chooses to accept an offer despite not earning a high wage, can we truly label them as exploited?[61]

I find Nozick's viewpoint persuasive. Marx's theory of exploitation suggests that capitalists always reap profits, but in reality, entrepreneurs also face losses. If adherents of Marx's theory argue for workers to share in profits during times of capitalist success, should they also bear losses during periods of capitalist failure? Moreover, in the 21st century, the likelihood of business failure far exceeds that of success, with studies showing that up to 90% of startups fail within five years. In such a context, many wage earners are likely reluctant to accept terms that involve sharing in losses. In contrast to Marx, Nozick contends that a significant portion of a commodity's value stems from the risk-taking behavior of capitalists, rather than solely from labor as Marx argued. Indeed, entrepreneurship and investment bear resemblances to gambling to some extent due to the complexities of markets, where even diligent efforts and full deployment of talents offer no certainty of profitability.

Nozick views profits from investments and business ventures as rewards for the risks assumed by investors. In contemporary times, many skilled workers secure well-paying jobs and have the means to invest or start businesses. However, the number of high-income earners willing to venture into entrepreneurship remains scarce. If investing were risk-free and could guarantee profits, one might expect widespread entrepreneurship, but directly linking labor input and production effort to guaranteed profits in the capital market is unrealistic. In the 21st century, music distribution has shifted to digital and streaming formats. Even if one were to produce cassette tapes diligently today, it would likely yield little success, as cassette tapes are obsolete for this era. Work inherently involves exchanging labor for wages without assuming the risk of investment. Since workers consciously opt out of taking risks, they should accept the outcomes when capitalists succeed in their ventures. Many workers feel exploited and unfairly treated when they witness capital owners accumulating substantial profits while they continue to receive fixed wages.

Yet this sense of envy and regret comes from the inability to predict future outcomes accurately. Similarly, regret over purchasing insurance when no claims arise underscores the preventive nature of insurance as protection against unforeseen circumstances. The reason people buy insurance is precisely because they cannot predict what unexpected events may occur. To regret that decision afterward is pointless.

In a free market, the choice between taking investment risks and opting for secure employment is fair for everyone.

5. The Diversity and Inclusiveness of Capitalism

The Allegory of the Cave and The Age of Enlightenment

It is generally perceived that the turning point in the development of human civilization is the transition from ignorance to enlightenment, and from subjugation to authority to the pursuit of freedom. The ancient Greek philosopher Plato depicted this path of human progress through the allegory of the cave. Allow me to briefly recount Plato's allegory. Some humans are born and live in a cave without sunlight and cannot leave. They are bound, forced to look only at the cave wall. Behind them, others carry torches, casting shadows on the wall. For these cave dwellers, the cave is their entire world and all that they understand. The cave is comfortably temperate, with water and food, providing a tolerable existence.

One day, however, an individual among them discovers a way to free himself and gradually climbs out of the cave, seeing sunlight and a new world for the first time. Plato makes two key points about this story. First, once a cave dweller leaves the cave and sees the real world, it is impossible for him to return to cave life. Second, the person who escapes the cave will inevitably tell his former companions about the world outside and try to lead them out of the cave.[62]

This simple allegory vividly depicts the human journey from ignorance to enlightenment in just a few lines. Once people leave the cave and see the real world, realizing their previous environment was built on falsehoods, they will undoubtedly choose the truth. Moreover, living in the cave might seem comfortable, but leaving behind a familiar life requires courage. Once people achieve freedom, they are unlikely to return, even if freedom means enduring hardships like extreme weather or poverty.

Plato's allegory, written over 2, 000 years ago in ancient Greece, captures a crucial moment in human history. However, it took humanity over a thousand more years to truly leave the metaphorical cave. During this period, both Eastern and Western civilizations were confined within the boundaries of religion and social norms, limiting their understanding of the world. In Europe, for instance, it was not until the Renaissance in the 15th century, followed by the Reformation and the Enlightenment, that people truly embraced scientific rationality and humanistic values. Before this, society in the Middle Ages in Europe was dominated by religious authority. Society valued collective norms over individual rights and desires. The Catholic Church defined societal values, dictating what was right and wrong. Divergent views were considered heretical and often brought suppression or even death upon those who expressed them, as seen when the Italian philosopher Giordano Bruno was executed by the Catholic Church in 1600, because of his beliefs in the theory of heliocentrism proposed by Copernicus.

This is not to completely denounce Christian or Catholic doctrines. In fact, I recognize that concepts like universal brotherhood within these doctrines have become central to modern Western values, such as equality for all people. However, the Catholic Church's effort to eliminate conflicting values and restrict individual expression significantly hindered human civilization's progress. Even after the Middle Ages, when religious influence waned and individual freedoms increased, their authority's impact did not disappear entirely. Monarchical power based on the same principles and structures replaced religious authority, and wealth and power remained concentrated among the elite. Subsequent historical events, such as the French Revolution at the end of the 18th century and the Russian Revolution in the early 20th century, were reactions against monarchical power by the lower classes.

As history progressed, humanity gradually discarded authority, left the cave, and embraced more humane values like freedom and equality. Thoughts and values were no longer confined by a single doctrine, and the concept of a universally correct standard dictated by authority vanished. People gained more freedom to innovate according to their ideas. What was once a privilege reserved for the nobility became a fundamental right for everyone in modern society in the western world.

Brief History of Modern Economics

If we reflect on the development of modern Western economics, we can see a similar journey out of the cave. The pivotal moment when economic thought emerged from the cave was with the publication of Adam Smith's *The Wealth of Nations*. At the outset of this book, Adam Smith is recognized as the father of modern capitalism due to his introduction of the "invisible hand" concept. He argued that economic development decisions should be decentralized and left to the market and private sector, as this is what drives national economic growth. However, prior to this, the prevailing economic thought in Europe was markedly different. Before the 18th century, economic activities were heavily influenced by the state and the monarchy, during a period known by economic historians as Mercantilism.

To the rulers of European countries at that time, improving the living standards of ordinary citizens was not the primary objective of economic development. Instead, they focused on strengthening the nation and its military. Precious metals like gold were highly valued because they enabled countries to purchase necessary goods from abroad and issue domestic currency. Trade between nations was seen as a zero-sum game, meaning there was always a winner and a loser in every transaction. Mercantilist proponents generally believed that sellers typically profited from trade, making buyers the disadvantaged party in most cases. As a result, European countries sought to maximize their exports to obtain precious metals while minimizing imports to conserve these metals for future needs.

Influenced by mercantilism, rulers preferred to concentrate wealth among the upper echelons of society, such as the nobility. Certain industries and land ownership were monopolized by the upper class. For rulers, this approach had two main benefits: it facilitated the centralization of resources to respond quickly to emergencies like wars, and it secured the support of the nobility to maintain social stability. To achieve this, economic activity among the lower classes had to be kept relatively subdued.

The Profound Impact of *The Wealth of Nations* on Economics

The release of *The Wealth of Nations* fundamentally changed the perception of national economic development in Europe. Adam Smith's work argued for enriching the populace as the primary economic goal. By allowing market freedom and providing opportunities for individuals to pursue wealth, overall productivity would be unleashed. This economic activity, according to Smith, defines true national wealth, and a thriving economy would naturally increase state revenue through taxes.

Smith also refuted the idea that trade is a zero-sum game, asserting that trade benefits both parties. Sellers gain profits, while buyers can use purchased goods for further production or to personally enjoy them, deriving greater value from them than their initial cost. Smith further argued that precious metals are not a true measure of national wealth, likening such hoarding to storing useless rocks.

The Wealth of Nations was revolutionary, showing that individuals do not need kings or nobles. In a free market, people can achieve happiness and wealth through their own efforts, and since economic transactions benefit all involved, they contribute to societal value and morality.

Capitalism's triumph is evident from the wealth surge in 19th-century Britain and beyond. Although proponents of capitalism emphasize the importance of market freedom and limited government interference, they can struggle with how to maintain social justice and equality. Capitalism is not perfect and has faced criticism over the centuries. While the free market's status has varied globally, with some nations embracing it fully and others modifying or rejecting it, historically, capitalist nations tend to be more advanced, both materially and morally. In the 21st century, capitalism and free markets are the dominant systems worldwide.

The Evolution of Capitalism in Modern Society

In response to criticisms by advocates for justice and equality, libertarian capitalists have continually adapted the system, incorporating various other ideas. In the 17th century, John Locke emphasized fundamental human rights and personal freedoms within the socio-economic system, rarely addressing issues like income inequality. Two centuries later, John Stuart Mill, another British philosopher, also emphasized individual freedom but differed from Locke by integrating concepts of justice and equality into liberalism. Historically, Mill's ideas laid the groundwork for incorporating egalitarianism into the free market.

Nonetheless, the 20th century saw persistent criticism of the free-market system's ability to be egalitarian. Especially in the latter half of the century, many Western left-wing scholars sympathized with and looked to the Soviet and Chinese models. While mainstream academia generally agrees on the necessity of balancing freedom and equality within capitalism, there remains ongoing debate about the exact proportions and methods for achieving this balance. Questions as to whether freedom or equality is more important, whether welfare should be implemented, or whether the government should intervene in the market are all part of this discussion. The varying balances and combinations of freedom and equality have led to diverse definitions of modern liberalism. There are reportedly over 30 academic definitions of liberalism based on these differing balances and implementation methods.

Among the numerous debates about liberalism in the 20th century, the most notable is that between John Rawls and Robert Nozick. Their views on the balance of equality and freedom in a capitalist system and on how to make capitalism more just are among the most extreme, though on opposite ends of the spectrum. This debate is a significant example of the diversification process within capitalism.

Redistribution of Wealth Makes Society Fairer?

John Rawls [63], as I interpret his work, supports the core tenets of capitalism, such as the protection of private property and the principles of free market competition. Nonetheless, he strongly advocates incorporating elements of equality into the free market system. If we liken economic development to a pie, Rawls believes that market mechanisms are the best way to enlarge the pie. However, he is primarily concerned with how the pie should be distributed. He opposes the communist notion of equal distribution, arguing that since individuals contribute differently to making the pie, equal distribution would be unfair and demotivating for hard workers. On the other hand, distributing the pie based solely on individual contributions is also problematic for Rawls. It is difficult to accurately assess and quantify each person's contribution, especially for those who contribute indirectly. Additionally, this approach could leave less capable individuals with too little and highly talented individuals with more than they need. Thus, Rawls argues that a proportional distribution solely based on contribution is not genuinely fair either.

Rawls believes that the difficulty lies in reaching an objective standard for how much pie each person should get, resulting in subjective judgments driven by personal interests. Every market participant has their own biases, making true fairness and justice hard to achieve. Therefore, he suggests the need to draft a fair distribution agreement with an unbiased and neutral perspective. However, this idea seems counterintuitive to many. According to Adam Smith, people are inherently self-interested and consider issues from their own perspectives.

Rawls and the Veil of Ignorance

John Rawls contends that fair distribution is feasible and introduces the concept of the *"Veil of Ignorance"*. The Veil of Ignorance suggests that, when making ethical decisions, we should envision ourselves behind a curtain that eliminates all personal stances and prejudices. For example, when determining the distribution of wealth in an economy, some might propose heavy taxes on the rich to subsidize the poor. Such a proposal would likely be welcomed by the poor and dismissed by the rich, due to their inherent biases.

Rawls believes that the Veil of Ignorance can be implemented in three steps. First, we should imagine a veil that separates us from the world. Behind this veil, we possess no personal characteristics. We must envision ourselves without any stance, gender, race, class, property, or religious beliefs. Rawls calls this state the "Original Position" and argues that, from the Original Position, we can evaluate the fairness and justice of distribution without the influence of personal biases.

In the second step, once we enter the Original Position, we must imagine ourselves as one of the parties affected by the policy and determine if we would be satisfied with the situation. For example, referring back to the tax example, we can imagine that if we were poor, we would likely agree with the policy since it would raise our standard of living. However, we also need to consider the perspective of the rich. For the wealthy, heavy taxation might feel like a loss of part of their income. Nonetheless, providing financial stability to the poor can contribute to a more stable society, allowing the rich to invest in a secure environment. On the other hand, the rich often undertake higher-risk jobs and investments and are uncertain about how long their current income will last. Establishing a system that protects the purchasing power of the poor might also be viewed as a form of insurance.

In the final step, we remove the Veil of Ignorance and sign a contract based on the drafts created behind the veil. After signing, no one in society can modify or regret the contract. If a distribution system can be designed behind the veil that all parties can accept, Rawls would consider this to be a completely fair, just, and rational policy.

The Two Principles of the Best Society

Rawls contends that a system designed by removing societal biases through the use of the Veil of Ignorance would typically enshrine two principles of justice. The first is the *"Principle of Equal Basic Liberties"*. This principle, akin to classical liberalism, states that everyone should have equal freedoms, such as freedom of speech and religious belief. Moreover, private property rights should be respected and protected from infringement. According to Rawls, equal liberty is a universal value, and no one has a reason to reject these rights. Behind the Veil of Ignorance, individuals would not want their hard-earned wealth taken away, nor would they want to live in fear or disapproval due to their religious beliefs. Likewise, when a rational individual desires their own freedom behind the Veil of Ignorance, they must also agree to others having the same rights. Consequently, Rawls accepts fundamental market economy mechanisms like free competition and the protection of private property.

Theory of Justice	Principles	Definition
First Principle	Equal Basic Liberties	Each person should have as much liberty as possible, as long as others have the same
Second Principle	Fair Equality of Opportunity	Inequality permitted, as long as, they relate to positions open to all under equality of opportunity
	Difference Principle	Inequality permitted, as long as, they are for the greatest expected benefit of the least advantaged members of society

The first principle is straightforward; the main controversy surrounding Rawls's theory related to his second principle. Although Rawls recognizes the importance of free competition in economic operations and accepts the resulting income inequality, he proposes that the outcomes of such inequality must satisfy two conditions. The first condition is *"Fair Equality of Opportunity"*, which argues that while income may be unequal, everyone in society should have equal rights to pursue their goals and compete for high-paying jobs. For example, high-income professions like doctors or lawyers are generally very popular. This condition asserts that anyone who wants to become a doctor or lawyer should have the opportunity and qualifications to study law or medicine. However, Rawls believes that mere equality of opportunity is insufficient.

If competition is only formally open to everyone, this represents mere *"Formal Equality"*. Rawls argues that even with open competition for professions like lawyers or doctors, competitive advantages are often skewed towards certain groups due to factors like family wealth, residential areas, and the quality of primary and secondary education.

In Taiwan, for example, students from the Xinyi District are overrepresented at National Taiwan University, suggesting that those from wealthy families in Xinyi have a higher chance of attending NTU. If Rawls noticed this phenomenon in Taiwan, he would argue that although the education system superficially guarantees equal opportunities for all to attend NTU, the different starting lines for wealthy individuals, such as their ability to afford private tutoring, undermine true equality of opportunity. Therefore, Rawls would likely advocate for leveling the playing field by providing identical education to all students to achieve truly fair and equal competition, which those behind the Veil of Ignorance would endorse. Hence, fair equality of opportunity is the first condition of Rawls' second principle.

Despite our best efforts to eliminate competitive advantages gained after birth, inherent differences between individuals remain. Some individuals are naturally gifted in their professions, while others, regardless of their efforts, cannot reach the same level of proficiency. When these two types of individuals compete, the former is more likely to win, which, according to Rawls, still does not constitute equality of opportunity.

This leads us to the second condition of Rawls's second principle: *"The Difference Principle"*. Rawls argues that those who gain a market advantage due to innate intelligence and talent have an obligation to share part of their wealth with the least advantaged members of society. Rawls believes that to address the inequalities arising from free competition, the winners must redistribute some of their income to improve the conditions of the most disadvantaged individuals. Those behind the Veil of Ignorance would naturally worry about becoming the least advantaged at some point, too. Therefore, without ensuring that the lowest class of society can improve, the inequalities produced by free competition would be unjust.

Rawls's Veil of Ignorance framework, as well as his two principles, allow for competition within a capitalist system and the mechanisms of a free market. However, it is essential that everyone has equal access to competitive opportunities and that even those who fail in competition receive social support to prevent their living standards from declining. Clearly, Rawls's logic supports a welfare society that imposes heavy taxes on the wealthy and redistributes the revenue to the lowest class of society to ensure a minimum standard of living.

Income Redistribution Equivalent to Expropriation?

Another American philosopher, Robert Nozick, completely disagrees with Rawls's claims. Although both philosophers fall within the liberalism spectrum, they occupy opposite extremes. Nozick argues that the idea represented by the Veil of Ignorance, which requires the wealthy to forcibly share part of their property with the least advantaged in society, is akin to robbery.

From Nozick's perspective, while Rawls accepts the primary operational principles of capitalism, he fails to fully respect individual rights when it comes to wealth distribution.[64] Particularly in Rawls' second principle of justice, the idea that those with competitive advantages have an obligation to improve the conditions of the least well-off lacks logical consistency. For example, if a woman cannot find a job due to her unattractive appearance, should more attractive women be obliged to subsidize her cosmetic surgery? Or, if two university students, Student A and Student B, interview for the same job and only Student A is hired, should Student B, as the unsuccessful candidate, be entitled to compensation from Student A? These examples might seem extreme, but logically they are consistent with Rawls's theory of justice.

Nozick: Justice Lies in Legitimate Acquisition of Wealth

Nozick emphasizes that individual freedom and rights are of utmost importance and should not be violated. This viewpoint is commonly known as libertarianism. He sets forth two principles concerning the functioning of capitalist systems and free markets. The first principle is that individual rights must be absolutely prioritized and must not be infringed upon. The second principle is that the free market should not be subject to government intervention under any moral justification. These principles clearly show that Nozick is a staunch supporter of capitalism. Unlike mainstream economists, Nozick has no interest in capitalism's ability to create wealth. He supports a market economy solely because he believes it is the most just system.[65]

Rawls argues that once wealth is created in society, we should consider how to distribute it as justly as possible. In contrast, Nozick believes that as long as a person's method of acquiring wealth is legal, moral, and free from coercion or fraud, they have no obligation to share their wealth with others. Public authorities have no right to interfere. Regarding income inequality, Nozick argues that redistribution should only be through voluntary donations, as this is the only way for the wealthy to contribute willingly. Any form of compulsory taxation and welfare programs is, in Nozick's view, morally unacceptable.

Capitalism Is Continually Evolving

In the 21st century, when we discuss the concept of liberalism, it has evolved significantly from its roots in classical liberalism. The liberalism that John Locke introduced in the 17th century was more straightforward, advocating for individual freedom and rights. Over the past few centuries, however, liberalism has faced persistent criticism from egalitarian perspectives and has incorporated elements related to equality, continually evolving. In the United States, the term "liberal" has even become associated with left-wing ideologies.

Despite the integration of egalitarian concepts into modern liberalism, it remains fundamentally liberalism, not egalitarianism. In my opinion, when freedom and equality clash, we must prioritize freedom, placing equality second. Reflecting on the debate between Nozick and Rawls, while I find Nozick's views too extreme and entirely rejecting social welfare impractical, the principle of prioritizing freedom over equality should guide us. People have different talents and abilities and contribute differently to wealth creation. Enforcing equality without considering these contributions is unreasonable and goes against human nature. It is fair to reward those who work harder, have greater talent, and make more significant contributions.

Moreover, history demonstrates that attempts to achieve fairness through government intervention often lead to unintended consequences. Even well-intentioned policymakers can succumb to corruption without proper oversight. The corruption issues in the Soviet Union and China are telling examples. Ultimately, we must acknowledge that the most effective way to generate wealth is through the capitalist free-market system. We should focus on increasing wealth before discussing its distribution. Ignoring wealth creation and focusing solely on distribution will result in historical tragedies and farcical outcomes.

As I write this, I recall a quote from U.S. President Benjamin Franklin: "Those who would give up essential Liberty, to purchase a little temporary Safety, deserve neither Liberty nor Safety".[66]

6. Capitalism in Future Society

Human technology is progressing at an unprecedented pace. Not long ago, we were amazed at how big data could uncover business insights and forecast future trends. Today, artificial intelligence (AI), with its extraordinary computational power, can outplay top human Go players. With the advent of ChatGPT 3.0 in 2023, AI has shown its ability to write poetry, create art, and inspire human creativity. ChatGPT's capabilities illustrate that AI can not only organize and process vast amounts of existing information but also create new, original content.

In the 20th century, economists like Mises, Hayek, and Keynes pondered the feasibility of planned economies and communism, focusing on how to collect all necessary information from society to make accurate predictions. The consensus among mainstream economists was that it was beyond human capability to gather enough social data to control the economy. Even if future technology could provide all market data, it could not predict individual preferences and innovate solely through technological and governmental intervention.[67]

Yet, the rapid technological advancement over the past century likely surpassed their wildest dreams. This has led many to wonder if AI, with its ability to accurately track individual actions, make precise predictions, and foster economic and social advancement, could soon be able to address the problem of information scarcity that previous communist states faced, thereby enabling the realization of true communism by planned economy..

Traditional View on Planned Economies

In Marx's view, free markets, price mechanisms, private property, and currency are all sources of economic turmoil, and these institutions will ultimately disappear along with capitalism.[68] Marx suggested in his writings that capitalism would be replaced by an administrative body organized by social elites, which would plan and execute economic activities through public authority. I interpret this to mean Marx believed that if production decisions were made by the government rather than individuals in the market, there would be no overproduction or waste. Similarly, if prices were set by public authority rather than merchants, economic crises could be avoided, eliminating the need for market self-regulation. Such a planned economy would be more stable and bring society closer to achieving social justice.

Marx's critique of capitalism was not without merit. In the context of the extreme income inequality of the 19th century, his criticisms actually spurred to create a subject and enable the active voice for self-reflection within the free market system. However, his idea of using public authority to replace market mechanisms for production and distribution has faced significant criticism. Even if we set aside the question of whether a planned economy can truly achieve justice, scholars like Hayek argue that the idea of public authority controlling and utilizing all market information is far-fetched and impractical.

A Planned Economy Is Bound to Encounter an Information Problem

Hayek contends that any advocates of a planned economy who endeavor to bring this system to fruition inevitably face the Knowledge Problem.[69] He means that, even if in the future, humanity could gather all behavioral data from society, state authorities could not replace the market in making production and consumption decisions, as Marx envisioned. This is because much of the necessary market knowledge cannot be captured through concrete data or language, which is the essence of the Knowledge Problem.

Consider a vendor planning to open a food stall in Taipei's night market. The vendor has various cuisine options, such as soup noodles, Chinese pancakes, or salted porridge. The choice depends on the existing stalls and the customer demographics. Additionally, flavor adjustments might be necessary since southern Taiwanese prefer sweeter flavors compared to the north.

According to Hayek, these crucial business decisions cannot be derived merely from data or logical analysis. He describes this as *Tacit Knowledge*.[70] Entrepreneurs need to immerse themselves in a specific industry or market to acquire the insights and tacit knowledge vital for success. This type of knowledge is abstract, difficult to express and reflect in data. These business insights are acquired through the market's repeated operations. For example, a vendor might only realize that customers at the night market dislike beef noodles or that the food quality is inadequate after receiving feedback. Using state authority and data to predict and immediately obtain the correct conclusion is impossible, in Hayek's view. While sales and profit data for various foods can be collected, the skill of adjusting flavors is something only the vendor can understand and master. This is akin to Lao Tze's saying: "The immortal rule cannot be told". These principles, which can only be grasped intuitively, are best left to the market.

In historical instances where planned economies were implemented, the elites responsible for economic planning invariably encountered the Knowledge Problem. Rather than producing goods genuinely needed by the populace, these planners often resorted to "blind guessing" or fulfilling "political mandates" from higher authorities. Bureaucrats working in isolated offices were incapable of understanding the actual needs of farmers in remote regions. Consequently, they relied on crude mathematical models to predict demand and guide production. This rigid execution of planned economies often led to mismatch of demand and demand, and therefore also poverty, scarcity, and even famine.

Regarding the Knowledge Problem, Hayek famously stated that no one, except the market itself, can determine how many pairs of white socks will be needed next year.[71]

Technology and AI Make a Planned Economy Feasible?

In recent years, the rapid pace of technological advancement has reignited interest in the nearly obsolete ideals of planned economies and communism. As previously discussed, market information can be divided into data and knowledge. While data may be readily available to governments, commercial knowledge is much harder to obtain. However, advancements in technology, particularly in artificial intelligence (AI), suggest that AI may soon be able to acquire better commercial knowledge and insights than humans. This raises the possibility that AI could make economic decisions more efficiently than individual market participants.

The advent of Big Data technology demonstrates that it is possible to collect and process vast amounts of data in various formats. Theoretically, if hardware capabilities are sufficient, all commercial behavior data in the market can be gathered and analyzed. Historically, predicting future market demands has been challenging, but Big Data may enable us to anticipate consumer needs more accurately. However, Big Data primarily relies on historical data for predictions and cannot drive societal progress and innovation. For example, before the iPhone's launch in 2007, even with Big Data technology, predictions would likely have favored Nokia's continued growth, without accounting for Apple's game-changing smartphone innovation that significantly diminished Nokia's market share.

Can AI Solve the Knowledge Problem?

The swift advancement of AI has transformed our understanding of technology. In 2023, the release of ChatGPT, with its remarkable computational and language processing abilities, stunned the world. There are two key distinctions between AI technology and previous Big Data technology. First, AI has self-learning capabilities. Big Data operations depend entirely on human-fed data to make predictions. In contrast, AI not only processes this data but also learns from previous outcomes, improving its performance over time. This means that even if human progress stalls, AI will continue to grow stronger as it operates (*Machine Learning*).[72]

Second, unlike Big Data, AI, as demonstrated by ChatGPT, exhibits creativity.[73] We can engage in spontaneous conversations with AI, and it can respond adeptly to new and imaginative questions. Furthermore, AI can take minimal information and produce written letters, drawings, or even novels. From the limited input we provide, ChatGPT can naturally infer context and enhance the content to create a complete and original work.

I am not here to promote modern technology, but it is hard not to consider the future of our capitalist economy when we see the advancements in technology. Hayek's critique of planned economies, particularly his knowledge problem, raises the question of whether future technology could resolve these issues. AI might be able to understand complex business insights and knowledge that are difficult to articulate. Instead of business owners figuring out how to start a night market business through trial and error, AI could provide quick and effective recommendations, such as what type of food to sell and how to season it to attract customers.

Hayek believed that economic progress and wealth creation require positive competition in the market, but this belief might be challenged in a future with advanced AI. As mentioned earlier, AI can continually learn and improve, potentially becoming even more creative in the future. If advanced AI had existed before 2007, it might have suggested adding internet access, video streaming, music playback, and touchscreens to Nokia phones, possibly preventing Nokia's market share collapse.

Hayek argued that government bureaucrats cannot understand the needs of every market participant and cannot incentivize progress without competition, thus necessitating a free market and making planned economies unfeasible. However, AI challenges this theory. If bureaucrats, using AI, could accurately determine the needs of a night market or predict the demand for white socks next year, or foresee the need for smartphones during Nokia's peak, the principle that freedom is essential for economic development could be challenged. If AI can more efficiently understand and communicate business insights than the market, the government might not need a free market to drive economic development. In other words, the government would not need the expertise of an Italian cuisine vendor to open an Italian restaurant, nor the innovation of Apple to create a smartphone; state-owned enterprises could achieve these tasks with the guidance of AI.

Our Society Will Still Need Capitalism

To understand where capitalism might be headed in the future, we should consider trends in human economic and social development. From my perspective, two economic trends are likely to emerge. First, our economic system will become increasingly complex, making it more difficult to control. As the economy grows, the variety of goods and services needed by people will increase, leading to more diverse job roles and more varied forms of collaboration among people. A century ago, China was still a predominantly agrarian society, with most people working in agriculture. It would have been hard to imagine jobs like assembling iPhones at Foxconn or analyzing data at Amazon to boost web traffic.

As economic systems grow more complex, they become harder to manage. During the Soviet era, the government strictly enforced a planned economy, simplifying economic activities to maintain control. There was only one type of butter and one type of soap, as this was the only way to implement production plans and a command economy. Despite this simplification, the Soviet Union still faced chronic shortages under its planned economy. In Western capitalist societies, attempts to control complex economic systems have not been particularly successful. The numerous economic crises of the 20th century and the inconsistent monetary policies of various countries suggest that we know too little to effectively manage complex systems. Although technology and artificial intelligence are advancing rapidly, the concurrent exponential increase in economic complexity makes it difficult to say that AI will be able to replace the market and control the economy in the future.

Second, and more importantly, human values will continue to underpin societal development. Humanism and universal values will remain predominant, which conflicts with the idea of AI replacing the free market or creating an AI-driven command economy. The engine driving economic progress is not monetary policy or GDP, but rather the human spirit. It is the human desire for material wealth, happiness, and meaning that drives economic activities through market exchanges. Essentially, controlling the economy equates to controlling human motivations.

I am unsure if future AI will be capable of understanding and predicting human nature comprehensively, but it is currently very difficult for AI to interpret human emotions and thoughts through behavior. Achieving this in the short term seems improbable. Humans change their minds quickly and are skilled at hiding their true feelings.

On an economic scale, events like stock market declines causing public panic or consumer responses to new products are driven by numerous unpredictable individual emotions. I doubt that AI can accurately predict these phenomena yet.

Technology to Replace Capitalism?

Even if artificial intelligence could theoretically replace market mechanisms and the government could create a utopian society through AI, this would be incompatible with humanistic ethics and universal values. Technology and the economy are fundamentally different. Technology is developed by a select group of intelligent individuals, with complexities beyond the understanding of the general public, and is controlled by societal elites. However, the economy is fundamentally driven by the decisions of every individual in society. Society is composed of a wide variety of people with different personalities, values, and preferences. Yet, within the market, they must respect one another and provide mutual value to create a functioning society.

Therefore, the idea of the government using AI to achieve economic development and social ethics, thereby replacing the capitalist system, essentially reflects the difference between centralization and decentralization, as well as between concentrated and dispersed power. Capitalism and the free market fundamentally represent the latter. In a capitalist system, decisions about the direction of economic development, the types of goods to be produced, and the services to be provided are made by individuals through market activities. This means that no single person can control these decisions. While the government may influence the overall direction, the final decisions are made by individuals.

In contrast, in the future, those who can understand, design, and control AI will likely always be a small elite group. Using AI to control economic activities could negatively impact our democratic system. Even though authorities may have good intentions in creating a better society through the use of a more efficient AI the fact that AI is controlled by a few people in power inherently predisposes it to power centralization. History tells us that humans have a desire for power, and when absolute power comes with benefits, we cannot guarantee it will not be abused. Once we give up the capitalist system and our economic decision-making power, it may be too late to reclaim.

Thus, capitalism will not and should not be abolished even in future societies. Joi Ito, in his book *Whiplash*, [74] asserts that with the increasing complexity and unknowns of future economic collaboration, economic development will rely more on market emergence rather than central control and authority. Emergence refers to the phenomenon where independent elements come together to form a higher-level entity, invoking the expression, "two heads are better than one". In large companies, individual employees might be ordinary, but collectively, they can create transformative enterprises like Amazon or Apple through collaboration and idea exchange.

Applying this concept to the market and society, readers will see that emergence resembles Adam Smith's "invisible hand". Each market participant may perform simple tasks, unaware of their overall contribution. However, as everyone works diligently, society as a whole unknowingly advancing toward greater path of progress. As economic collaboration becomes more complex, top-down authority cannot drive growth. Instead, allowing individuals the freedom to develop the economy from the bottom up is essential. Joi Ito suggests that emergence is not merely about the whole being greater than the sum of its parts; it can also create a more complex and innovative society.

Emergence is not a new concept; the market mechanism itself is an emergent phenomenon, integral to modern capitalism. As economic systems grow more complex, emergence will become increasingly crucial. Like the free market, its core principle is that individuals are the source of economic development. Granting them freedom to compete and collaborate is vital for progress and innovation. Emergence requires information exchange and mass communication among individuals, as well as a free environment and personal incentives for seamless cooperation. If emergence and humanistic values continue to be the dominant models of future economic development, the free market will persist, and we will still need the capitalist system.

Delegating economic management to technology essentially transfers the power of the masses to a small elite. This is not conducive to the development of a humanistic society.

Conclusion: Lessons from History

Over the last two hundred years, the capitalist system has faced ups and downs in modern society. The idea of the free market has been frequently criticized and dismissed by mainstream society, only to be repeatedly vindicated. Prior to the 18th century, governments emphasized national strength through trade and the accumulation of precious metals, believing that the primary goal of economic development was national power. It was thought that private citizens should not compete with the state for profit, and that wealth should be concentrated among the upper classes, thereby limiting private economic development.

Adam Smith, the father of modern capitalism, challenged this view by advocating for the opening of markets for free trade and the establishment of a legal system to stimulate economic growth and private wealth accumulation. In essence, Smith reversed the economic roles of government and the private sector. He argued that private wealth was more important than national wealth, and thus economic development should be driven by private markets, with the government playing a secondary role.

While capitalism and the free market can create significant wealth, the side effects such as income inequality led scholars like Karl Marx to propose planned economies as an alternative. Planned economies gained prominence, with communist countries like China, the Soviet Union, North Korea, and Cuba adopting this approach. Throughout most of the 20th century, even though many capitalist countries did not fully embrace planned economies, the influence of this system greatly impacted their free-market economies. Particularly after the global financial crisis of the 1930s, there was growing criticism of the instability of capitalism and market mechanism, with calls for government intervention and regulation to prevent future economic crises.

The concept of regulating and intervening in free markets was the mainstream approach in Western capitalist countries until the 1970s. The global oil crisis and stagflation during the 1970s left many nations struggling, which led to a renewed focus on the power of free markets. In the 1980s, U.S. President Ronald Reagan's supply-side reforms and British Prime Minister Margaret Thatcher's economic liberalization policies[75] underscored the strength of unregulated free markets. Meanwhile, economic reforms in Communist China were gaining momentum, alongside the fall of the Soviet Union and the liberalization of Eastern European economies. As a result, free markets and capitalism became the dominant global paradigms, sparking subsequent globalization and significant wealth generation.

Nevertheless, the global economic crisis of 2008 seemed to revert history to the 1930s, challenging the notion that humanity had discovered the optimal economic system. In response to this financial crisis, U.S. President Barack Obama took decisive action to rescue the market, implementing bailout policies to support struggling investment banks. Similarly, China, as a leading economic power, introduced a *four trillion-yuan stimulus package*[76] to stimulate the economy through monetary policy. The belief that free markets could self-regulate in times of crisis was suddenly set aside. Clearly, policymakers' reactions to the 2008 economic crisis weretinged with panic.

The core principles of the capitalist system include respect for individual freedom, allowance of self-interest, promotion of fair competition, and ownership of private property. However, the global economic crisis of 2008 revealed the fragility of this system. As a fundamental aspect of modern civilization, the free-market system we currently have is not guaranteed to persist; it is conceivable that capitalism could decline or even disappear in the future. Human history over the past five thousand years shows that our civilization has not always progressed smoothly; there have been frequent ups and downs: from the intellectual freedom of ancient Greece and the splendor of ancient Rome, to the religious oppression of the Middle Ages; from the era of prolific philosophers and musicians in Germany to the tyranny of the Nazi regime in the 20th century; from the first democratic republic in east Asia in 1911, to the communistic authoritarianism in China. These examples demonstrate that remnants of previous civilizations can vanish within decades. The same applies to the capitalist system, which, as a hallmark of modern civilization, necessitates dissemination and advocacy through education and public discourse to ensure society continues to develop towards prosperity and humanistic values.

The fragility of capitalism arises from two primary factors. First, capitalism and the free market propose that in repeated interactions, individuals must honestly create value for others to achieve the greatest long-term benefits. However, the pursuit of long-term benefits is not innate to everyone. Generally, only in a stable and optimistic economic environment are people willing to sacrifice short-term profit maximization for greater long-term benefits.

During economic downturns, when confidence in life and prosperity diminishes, short-term opportunism may seem a more rational choice, given the uncertain future. Another prerequisite for individuals to honestly pursue long-term profits is a robust legal system. When the judiciary regresses and perceptions of unfairness prevail, trust among people erodes, leading to abandonment of long-term pursuits or exit from the market. Hong Kong in the 2020s serves as a pertinent example.

The second point is that political interests often conflict with those of capitalism. In a free market, individuals determine how to produce and offer value, competing with other businesses. This decentralizes power to the private sector, which can be uncomfortable for democratically elected governments, as it implies less control and an unpredictable direction for society. This challenge is significant for democratic governments seeking reelection and even more so for authoritarian regimes. Therefore, public authorities are often tempted to intervene in the free market. For governments, social stability is crucial. When the economy is struggling and public discontent rises, governments are compelled to act to stabilize the market. While bailout policies aim to protect citizens from economic crises, they often disrupt market mechanisms.

In the best-case scenario, taxpayer money is used to save inefficient businesses, damaging market confidence. In the worst-case scenario, excessive money printing leads to inflation and mounting debt, thereby worsening economic problems. History shows that short-term government bailouts might alleviate immediate crisis impacts, but their long-term consequences are often harmful. Thus, we should limit public authorities' power to intervene in the economy, as an authoritarian government could severely harm the capitalist system.

In modern society, capitalism is not just about making money and accumulating wealth. The ultimate goal of societal development should be to create a society that emphasizes humanistic values. Viewing the promotion of capitalism merely as an endorsement of profit-making misses the deeper significance. Capitalism can promote humanistic values both socially and individually.

Human empathy typically extends only to those close to us, making it difficult to trust and engage economically with strangers. However, capitalism incentivizes cooperation with strangers, as it brings significant benefits, especially when supported by a fair legal system. To profit, individuals must create value for others. Capitalism, with self-interest and profit as the basis for interacting with strangers, fosters a more moral and humane society. Capitalism also provides the freedom to decide how to produce and live, with the free market guiding these decisions. Additionally, capitalism enables fair competition, where success depends on the price and quality of products and services, without special treatment based on personal identity.

Capitalism provides modern society with increased freedom and possibilities, enabling people to choose freely what to create, what to buy, what values to pursue, and how to live their lives. Gone are the days when kings, dictators, or religious leaders dictated how individuals should live.

Yet capitalism is not a perfect system that can solve all problems, and Marx's 19th-century critiques of capitalism included valid points; it is important to recognize the serious issues of income inequality and social polarization that unrestrained capitalism can cause. However, in response to challenges on issues of egalitarianism, capitalism has continuously evolved and improved. Income redistribution is a notable example; governments use taxation to ensure a minimum standard of living for their citizens, preventing the social tragedies of Marx's time.

The Nordic model of capitalism is an excellent example of this.[77] Moreover, many capitalist countries adjust their systems to ensure that everyone can compete fairly and have equal opportunities for employment, education, and access to social resources. These efforts aim to ensure that opportunities are not unduly influenced by factors such as race, gender, or background.

We must accept that achieving equality, whether in opportunities or outcomes, is challenging and nearly impossible. Historical evidence shows that equality of outcomes is unattainable, as illustrated by the failures of communist countries that attempted to achieve absolute equality through planned economies. Even equality of opportunity is, in my view, impossible to perfect. Despite efforts to create a level playing field and remove luck-related factors such as race, gender, or background, complete equality remains elusive. The key issue is the significant variation in people; some are intelligent, some are not; some are diligent, some are lazy; some enjoy art, while others prefer making money. In such a complex and diverse society, striving for equality of opportunity can itself be a form of inequality.

In my view, our goal should be justice, not equality. Both in human society and nature, most creation and progress come from a minority of people and things, as illustrated by the Pareto Principle.[78] This is true for national economic activities and corporate management. This explains why most of society's wealth is controlled by a few individuals. Some may view this as inequality and use it to criticize capitalism.

However, I see it as a natural law, reflecting the varying abilities, creativity, and efforts of individuals. Rather than questioning whether the capitalist system is fair, the more pertinent question is whether the distribution within capitalism is just. For instance, if one person earns more income and wealth than another, we should focus on whether they have broken the law, engaged in exploitation, or obtained special privileges without fair competition. If someone, through their talent and hard work, earns a higher income without violating laws or morals, is not this also a form of fairness?

In conclusion, capitalism is universal and is not defined differently depending on ideology or culture. The core of economics is human nature, and capitalism's operational rules align most closely with it. Regardless of nationality or gender, we all have self-interested tendencies and yearn for freedom and equality. These desires do not change based on our cultural backgrounds. The capitalist system uniquely satisfies our human needs while enabling us to create value for one another.

Former British Prime Minister Winston Churchill once famously said of democracy: "Democracy is the worst form of government, except for all the others".[79] This sentiment applies equally to capitalism. By considering the ups and downs of the free market economy over the past two hundred years, as well as the economic disasters resulting from humanity's overconfidence in its rationality, I hope that we can learn from history and avoid repeating its mistakes in the future.

Appendix A: What Is the Point of Studying Economics?

I was once asked by someone, "What is the benefit of understanding economics for the general reader?" Honestly, I found myself at a loss, unable to articulate a persuasive answer. Economics and market operations are all around us every day. We know economics happens arounds us, but we cannot see or touch it. To me, economics is a way of thinking that has changed how I view society and the world. However, it is not a hard skill that can guarantee immediate career advancement or financial gain. Hence, I found it difficult to provide a specific explanation.

Some believe that economics is a field about money and that studying it will make you rich. This view flatters economics but also greatly misunderstands it. Economics is more about human nature, observing how people make decisions to understand social operations. Money is merely a superficial aspect of economics, a unit of measure for human behavior. Ironically, there is a joke among economists that the worst-performing individual investors in the stock market are often economics professors. Rather than actively investing in the highly volatile stock market, economists might be more likely to analyze static charts and models. Some claim that understanding economics provides excellent conversation topics and enables high-level discussions. But trust me, I rarely encounter people discussing economic theories at social gatherings. If you want engaging conversation topics, I suggest reading novels; these might offer better opportunities to shine in social settings.

When many people think of economics, particularly macroeconomics, they immediately associate it with concepts like macroeconomic regulation, inflation, deflation, and productivity-driven GDP growth. For policymakers or central bank governors, part of their job is to steer the national economy. For them, understanding these economic theories is indispensable. However, for the majority of the public who will never engage in managing a country's markets and wealth, it is perhaps true that studying economics does not bring immediate practical benefits.

After my friend posed that question, I reflected on the usefulness of economics for a while. Although economics may not offer immediate, tangible benefits, I still believe it is a highly valuable field of study. Firstly, adopting an economic mindset can transform your understanding of societal operations. In other words, understanding economics can make you more insightful and allow you to see different issues more deeply. For example, when a typhoon hits and vegetable and meat prices soar, while the public may blame unscrupulous vendors, you might realize that the disaster caused crop failures, reducing supply. Vendors then have to pay higher prices to farmers, which results in increased prices for the consumer. When China's GDP has surged in recent years and the public has been awed by its economic prowess, someone who has studied economics might have observed that the proportion of government investment in China's GDP is high compared to other countries, indicating that high GDP growth is not directly linked to private wealth.

Moreover, China's substantial debt poses a risk in leveraging future wealth for GDP growth. On the other hand, Japan, despite claims of prolonged economic stagnation and the *"Lost Decades"*, has managed to hide wealth among its citizens, with the economic crisis of the early 1990s having little impact on basic living standards. While mainstream society often equates cash with wealth, your knowledge of monetary theory tells you that a banknote is just a piece of paper, its value backed by national sovereignty. Thus, during economic downturns, the central bank can increase the money supply to stimulate circulation. However, increasing the money supply does not equate to increased national wealth, as the quantity of goods and rate of productivity remain unchanged. For the public, money represents wealth, but for the central bank, it is merely a unit of measurement. When many attribute Africa's poverty to a lack of natural resources or low educational levels, you might recognize that the larger issue lies in the economic systems of those impoverished countries. Without a fair and just judicial system to protect private property, people are hesitant to engage in production, trade, and investment. This explains why Japan, despite lacking natural resources, is a leading economic power. While most people understand society through interpersonal relationships and intuition, economic thinking helps us comprehend the world through numbers and logic, often leading to new insights and perspectives.

The second benefit of understanding economics lies in its capacity to cultivate ethical judgment. While many perceive economics as a science or, at minimum, a relatively objective social science, I contend that it more closely resembles, requiring subjective judgment by its readers. For instance, in economic operations, the pursuit of equality raises questions: should equality be defined as equal earnings for all (equality of outcome), or should it acknowledge differential rewards based on effort (equality of opportunity)? When economic principles clash—such as freedom versus equality—prioritizing one over the other poses ethical challenges. Moreover, during economic crises, should governments prioritize short-term market rescue measures despite their potential long-term economic repercussions?

Contrary to popular belief, mainstream academia lacks consensus on various economic theories, including market failures, state-owned enterprises, interventionist policies, government size, and monetary policies, topics that have been fiercely debated for decades. Additionally, economic viewpoints do not neatly divide into left and right factions but span a spectrum akin to political ideologies. Engaging with economic debates sharpens readers' ability to discern moral complexities and balance ethical considerations.

Ultimately, for the general reader, the foremost utility of economics lies in shaping character and promoting a sense of well-being. Some argue that ignorance breeds contempt, as deeper understanding of societal mechanisms may introduce complexity and anxiety. Conversely, embracing knowledge may disrupt previously held certainties, a source of discomfort for some. This parallels Socrates's distinction between contented pigs and contemplative humans. Readers interested in economic discourse reject a life of passive contentment and instead seek enlightenment. Understanding economic news, often laden with technical jargon, requires practice, but it is accessible. Unraveling order from chaos demands effort—a process Socrates likened to the pangs of childbirth, signifying the birth of new understanding.

Life unfolds as a series of intellectual challenges, and curiosity remains the key to personal fulfillment—an enduring lesson gleaned from the study of economics.

Appendix B: The Origins of Modern Economics

The idea of a market economy or modern capitalism originated in Scotland. It is the birthplace of Adam Smith, the father of modern economics and author of *The Wealth of Nations*. While part of Europe, Scotland is located at the northern tip of Great Britain, quite distant from the continent. This geographic separation mirrors the unique role of Scottish philosophers during the Enlightenment. Scotland was influenced by Continental Enlightenment ideas, yet its thinkers maintained a different approach to reason, arguing that it should not overshadow life. Unlike the mainstream Enlightenment view, which sought universal truths through simple, mathematical laws and logical deduction, Scottish thinkers like David Hume believed this approach was impractical. They argued that all supposed causal relationships are actually empirical observations.

For instance, the phenomenon of water boiling at 100 degrees Celsius is simply based on repeated observations, and theoretically, this could change. Thus, when applying this principle to other phenomena, further real-life experimentation is necessary. In essence, human logical deduction is not entirely reliable. Scottish Enlightenment thinkers advocated for finding truth through life experiences, observation, and adapting to one's environment, rather than isolating oneself to deduce truths through pure reason.

The Wealth of Nations, often called the bible of economics, was written in Scotland in 1776 and reflects Scottish Enlightenment thought. Adam Smith, regarded as the father of modern capitalism, argued that economic development required freeing society from constraints. In 18th-century Europe, centralization and state power were emphasized, with economic policies favoring mercantilism, where states aimed to export more than they imported to accumulate gold.

This system, controlled by the elite, restricted individual innovation and economic growth, benefiting vested interests. Adam Smith countered this by advocating for the removal of all trade restrictions and economic privileges. He believed the market, composed of independent individuals and businesses, functions best when individuals have the freedom to observe society and decide what to produce. The market is complex and cannot be fully understood by government agencies, hence should not be interfered with.

Smith suggested that allowing individuals the freedom to trade and produce would ensure maximum benefits for all and lead to societal progress. He described the market mechanism as an "invisible hand", where individuals pursuing their own interests would naturally drive economic advancement without causing chaos. However, he stressed the need for government to protect private property and ensure a fair judicial system, enabling the market to operate without fear of confiscation. According to Adam Smith, the market mechanism, or invisible hand, is the best way to achieve economic prosperity, fairness, and social order.

Adam Smith changed economic thinking and reshaped how policymakers manage national economies. This transformation had a significant and far-reaching impact on Europe and the world. The publication of *The Wealth of Nations* in the late 18th century and the spread of capitalist ideas led to unprecedented economic prosperity in 19th-century Europe, exemplified by the Industrial Revolutions in the UK and the US. In my opinion, the material progress in Europe beginning in the 19th century is closely tied to the capitalist market economy. Before the 19th century, economic development in human societies swung between extreme laissez-faire economics and strict regulatory control. Modern capitalism found a balance between these extremes. The beauty of capitalism lies in its dual nature: it allows individuals to freely pursue competition and wealth creation through market mechanisms while also requiring public authorities to ensure fairness, enabling people to confidently seek wealth.

Capitalism's impact extends beyond material wealth, inadvertently fostering humanistic progress through the market economy's development. For example, material progress led to the emergence of a relatively affluent middle class in European society. As the middle class accumulated wealth, they naturally sought greater political influence to protect their property. By securing political influence, the middle class ensured their freedom to pursue wealth and their right to equal treatment, contributing to the realization of humanistic values in society. Additionally, the 19th century also saw a significant artistic leap. Romantic music and Impressionist painting reached their artistic peak during this period and greatly influenced 20th-century modern art. It can be said that the development of art is closely related to capitalism. The material abundance brought by the capitalist market economy gave people more disposable income and leisure to appreciate art. Since people earn more money and basic needs are met, they can spend extra money and time on art and leisure.

Let us revisit the idea of reforming economic systems through rational thought. In the 19th century, the capitalist market economy was seen as the most effective system for creating wealth, leading to a significant increase in wealth in Europe and the United States. However, many people at the time believed that capitalism was not perfect, and some strongly opposed the system. Some scholars noted that the market mechanism was slow to self-correct during economic crises, that unemployment was a common issue, and that distrust among individuals could hinder trade. These points highlighted the market's shortcomings. From a social and humanistic perspective, some elites argued that capitalism conflicted with humanistic values, pointing out issues like income inequality resulting from free competition, monopolies, and the high cost of essential services like education and healthcare in an unregulated market. For these critics, the market was disorderly and incapable of achieving humanistic goals on its own. They argued that instead of letting the market develop freely, we could use reason to improve the market or even design a new system that better aligns with humanistic values.

Reforming economic systems through reason, as discussed earlier with psychology and society, involves incorporating mathematics into market theory to make economics resemble a science. During the late 18th century, when Adam Smith was active, academic disciplines were not as specialized as they became after the 20th century, and economics was not seen as an independent field. Many scholars who contributed to economics, such as Jeremy Bentham and John Stuart Mill, considered themselves philosophers rather than economists. Adam Smith used philosophical methods to think about wealth creation and distribution rather than scientific methods. After Smith introduced modern capitalist theories like the market mechanism and the invisible hand, the development of economics progressed rapidly.

Over the next century, economic theory integrated concepts from the natural sciences to explain market phenomena, leading to a more comprehensive understanding of economic operations and the development of modern economic theory. By the late 19th century, scholars like Léon Walras and Alfred Marshall began incorporating mathematical equations into economics, emulating physics. From that point on, mathematics replaced philosophy as the main method for understanding social market economic phenomena. By the 21st century, the prevalence of mathematical equations and graphs in textbooks often makes it seem like one is reading a physics book.

Even those with a limited background in economics have likely heard the story: all goods and services in the market have their own supply and demand, which determines their prices. When supply goes up, resulting in more production, prices fall. Conversely, when demand increases, meaning more people want the product, prices rise. These forces interact to form prices, meaning neither buyers nor sellers can arbitrarily set prices. This theory, introduced by Léon Walras, explains how price mechanisms work to achieve market equilibrium.

The market theory developed by Adam Smith through philosophical paradigms is referred to as classical economics. The theories presented by Alfred Marshall using mathematics and science are known as neoclassical economics. In fact, the framework and analysis methods of neoclassical theory have become the foundation of modern mainstream economics. Today, modern economics is extremely mathematical, making meaningful economic analysis seem impossible without mathematical equations.

While the analytical methods differ, making neoclassical economics appear quite different from classical theory, it is essentially a continuation of classical theory rather than a rebuttal Both neoclassical and classical economists recognize the power of the market. The difference lies in neoclassical economists' efforts to theorize market mechanisms through various assumptions and use mathematical models to show that social welfare and wealth can be maximized under certain conditions. Alfred Marshall, a neoclassical economist, illustrated this in his 1870 work *Principles of Economics*. The below graph depicts the process by which supply and demand interact to form market prices. This well-known graph is familiar to those with basic economic knowledge and often introduces the workings of a market economy. Essentially, neoclassical economics does not oppose the free-market development mechanisms proposed by classical

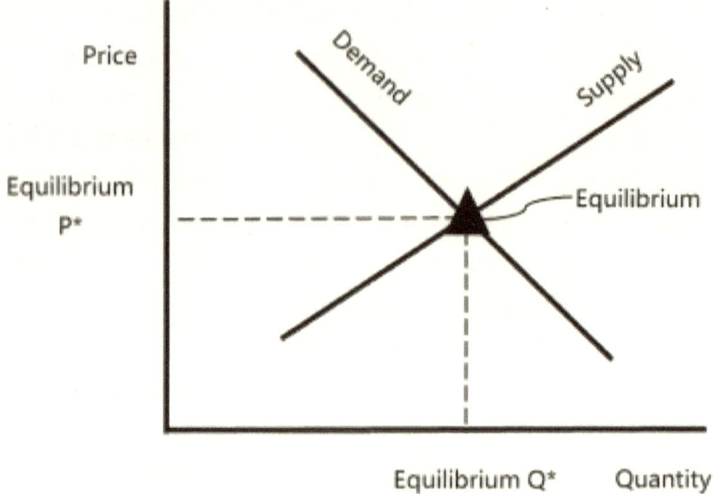

paradigms; it simply expresses Adam Smith's ideas in a different way.

The rise of the neoclassical school was like opening Pandora's box. Since then, mainstream economics has followed the path set by neoclassical economics, using its mathematical formulas and theories as a framework for further modifications.

While neoclassical economics did not initially aim to deny the market economy's mechanisms, the mathematization of economics inadvertently became the foundation for rational optimist economists. This approach, using numbers and mathematical models to explain economics, gave later scholars the sense that economics is a science. Much like water evaporates at 100 degrees Celsius and freezes at zero degrees, if we can fully understand the market economy through reason, we can scientifically transform, influence, or intervene in the capitalist system. This thinking continues to be central to modern economic theory. Some have even completely rejected capitalism, advocating for the abolition of the market economy, a concept that was realized in the 20th century.

Proponents of rationally transforming economic systems to achieve humanistic ideals in society generally share a belief that public authority must play a role in the socio-economic sphere. They argue that human nature is inherently selfish; thus, our rationality requires an impartial government to enforce humanistic morals, improving on the free-market economy and compensating for what it cannot achieve.

Appendix C: Why Marxist Economics Is Destined to Fail

Even in the 21st century, Marxism continues to be one of the most hotly debated academic topics. Some people vehemently oppose Marxism, arguing that the deaths of millions in the 20th century, in attempts to achieve communist ideals, prove its fundamental flaws. On the other hand, some view Marxism as a visionary framework for the future of humanity, insisting that historical communist states like the Soviet Union, China, and Cambodia did not achieve true communism.

Marxism presents a worldview that spans economics, politics, and sociology, but its theoretical foundation lies in economics. Marx believed that the basic structure of human society is grounded in economic activities (the base), [80] and that society, morality, and law (the superstructure)[81] are determined and constructed on this economic base. This discussion will focus on the economic aspects of Marx's theory. In my view, the premises and logic of Marxist economics are flawed, absurd, and do not align with human nature, thus predestining Marxist economics to fail. Because of these foundational errors, Marxism has been impossible to implement successfully.

Marx: Capitalism Will Eventually Disappear

Karl Marx's core belief is that capitalism will ultimately vanish in the course of history. Marx argued that the labor, effort, and time of the working class (proletariat) are the only true sources of economic value. He dismissed market demand, entrepreneurial ventures, and creativity as sources of value. According to Marx's "Labour Theory of Value", when a capitalist sells a product in the market, the selling price surpasses the worker's wages, resulting in profit for the capitalist. This profit, termed "surplus value" by Marx, is viewed as exploitation, as all value is generated by laborers. Thus, the capitalist's appropriation of surplus value is deemed unjust. Marx compared capitalists to vampires, feeding on the labor of the working class. Nevertheless, he believed that laborers would eventually become aware of this exploitation, unite, and overthrow the capitalists, ending capitalism.

Marx's ideas may seem like a futuristic fable. However, the historical events of the 20th century have shown that his vision was an unachievable utopia. His theory of exploitation is fundamentally incorrect, as value creation in reality involves more than just laborers. Entrepreneurs and capitalists utilize their vision and knowledge to create new products and investment opportunities, investing their own capital at significant risk, and they should be rewarded with profit. Without the right direction and innovative ideas, mere labor cannot achieve the advancements of modern civilization. For over two millennia, for example, Chinese farmers have worked hard, yet China remained a peasant society with little progress in material, ideological, or civilizational terms.

Moreover, Marx was prejudiced against money and financial activities that did not involve labor. Throughout his works, Marx suggested that accumulating wealth through financial means was unjust. His disdain for capitalism stemmed from his belief that money lacked productive capability and that only laborers deserved to accumulate wealth. Marx considered income from interest and profit as unjust gains. Even in the 19th century, this view was considered outdated and conservative.

Marx and the Planned Economy

Furthermore, Marx advocated for the implementation of a planned economy in a communist society. He argued for the elimination of fundamental aspects of capitalism and the free market, such as private property, market-based transactions, prices, and even money. Marx perceived a significant difference and inherent conflict between the decision-making power of public authority and that of the free market. He believed public authority should have moral intentions and absolute power to create and manage a fair society. In contrast, the free market is driven by individuals competing for limited resources and profit. The conflict lies in the fact that public authority is altruistic, while the free market is self-interested. Marx also predicted that over time, public authority, being exercised by individuals, would inevitably become corrupt and align with market interests. As a result, a society focused solely on self-interest and competition would fall into chaos. Marxists view the market as chaotic, irrational, and prone to fostering divisive and antisocial ideologies.[82]

To resolve this, Marx suggested that the free market should be controlled and managed by a central, democratically elected authority, such as the government. This authority would plan and execute decisions on production, quantity, and pricing. This would eliminate competition for resources as all economic activities would be pre-arranged by the government. This concept is known as a planned economy. Marx believed that abolishing private property entirely was the true expression of democracy and freedom, as competition in a free-market forces people to work hard and face exploitation, preventing them from achieving true fulfillment. He optimistically envisioned that, with public ownership, the government would serve merely as a temporary institution to prevent competition. Once material abundance reached a level where competition was unnecessary, the planned economy and government would no longer be needed.[83] In essence, with extreme material abundance, everyone could get what they need without competing. In the 21st century, this vision appears highly utopian and even unrealistic.

Critique of the Planned Economy

Supporters of Marx and the concept of a utopian planned economy often fail to recognize the market's complexity. In the advanced capitalist society of the 21st century, millions of products are in circulation, necessitating complex divisions of labor and extensive human resources to produce. The key issue is that the market's complexity surpasses the capacity of any government or institution to control.

A Marxist planned economy is impractical. Firstly, the government cannot fully gather the necessary information for a planned economy. In such a system, the government must decide what to produce, how much to produce, who will produce it, and who will receive the products. Without market prices or free competition, the government relies on data and technology to predict total economic output and pricing. However, modern economies are too vast and complex for accurate predictions of all economic activities. For example, predicting the exact number of road bicycles needed next year or the demand for brown briefcases is impossible. In a free market, these decisions are decentralized to individual businesses, which make profit-driven decisions based on market conditions. History shows that decentralized free markets are more efficient than planned economies.

Additionally, planned economies lack free competition. After the government creates an economic plan, state-owned enterprises (SOEs) carry out production, facing no competitive pressures. In a free market, competition provides essential information. For instance, in a night market, a food stall that fails to offer good quality and affordable food will naturally see reduced profits or go out of business due to fierce competition. This way, intense competition ensures that poorly managed businesses make way for more efficient ones.

Both prices and competition serve as information providers in the free market. This information helps allocate resources efficiently, making production more effective—an advantage that planned economies lack.

The second reason planned economies are impractical is their inability to escape governance by individuals. When the government executes its plans without market feedback, it also acts as the overseer. For example, when civil servants implement government economic plans, even if errors are discovered, the lack of external oversight means that as long as they appease their superiors, they often avoid accountability. This often leads to corruption and personal rule. This is completely different from the free market. In the business sector, companies that make mistakes see reduced profits or go bankrupt. Employees who make mistakes are accountable to their superiors or face dismissal. If a supervisor fails to catch a subordinate's mistake, the team's performance suffers, leading to the supervisor's eventual dismissal. If the entire management performs poorly, company failure is inevitable. Therefore, relying solely on individual governance is unsustainable in the market.

Finally, the lack of innovation is another reason planned economies are impractical. Governments and state-owned enterprises tend to stick to existing production methods and traditional practices rather than pursuing new ideas or innovations. Without competition among enterprises, state-owned enterprises only need to complete their assigned tasks, with no pressure to innovate. Moreover, new production methods, though potentially more efficient, could lead to unemployment and social unrest, which planned economies strive to avoid. In contrast, continuous innovation is the only way to survive in the free market.

For the reasons outlined above, consider this analogy: a planned economy might be workable in the kitchen of a small restaurant. The head chef can plan ahead for what ingredients to buy, what dishes to prepare, and even dictate minute-by-minute actions of the staff. But applying this management style to a larger market is a different story.

The tasks in a kitchen, from preparing dishes to coordinating efforts, are relatively simple and can be planned in advance. Moreover, the menu remains fixed for the day, and the chef doesn't expect the cooks to innovate during their work, making management straightforward. Employees simply follow the chef's directives without needing to think about improvements. While a planned economy might work in a small restaurant, it fails on a large market scale. Unfortunately, Marx believed such an economy could work in society.

Marx's critique of capitalism is not entirely unfounded, but his writings lack a detailed blueprint for how his envisioned communist society should function. His proposals for a planned economy, including establishing a proletarian democracy, creating economic plans, and defining a materially abundant society, require interpretation from his works. This lack of clear execution guidelines partly explains why figures like Vladimir Lenin, who endorsed violent power seizures, and Mao Zedong, who believed in initiating revolution through rural land reforms, drew such different conclusions from Marx's ideas.

Marx was an imaginative, romantic, and idealistic figure. His theories, which advocate for the underprivileged, exude a strong sense of morality and humanism. However, when these theories are put into practice, they often encounter numerous issues. We must remember the historical costs associated with Marxism and remain cautious about implementing this flawed and unrealistic theory.

Afterwords and Acknowledgements

I began writing this book in early 2020, and it has taken nearly four years to complete. The writing process was not smooth. Throughout this period, numerous personal setbacks and professional frustrations repeatedly interrupted my writing progress, leading me to start and stop multiple times. There were moments when I even considered giving up writing. I often wished I could write in peace, surrounded by serene landscapes. It might have made the writing process more enjoyable.

My relationship with writing is truly a mix of love and hate. Sometimes, as night falls, I find myself staring at the screen for hours, overwhelmed by thoughts but unsure where to begin, which is incredibly frustrating. Yet, inspiration often strikes unexpectedly, and after periods of struggle, it brings a flood of ideas. This "flow", almost as if divinely inspired, brings me immense happiness and satisfaction. The creation of this book was the result of many such cycles of pain and joy. As Georg Hegel said, the purpose of life is akin to the sprouting of a seed. Writing makes me feel like an uncoiling seed, allowing me to experience vitality, understand my inner self and potential, and achieve self-realization.

However, completing this book would have been impossible relying solely on my efforts. Without following masters, predecessors, friends, and family, this work would not have been possible. The thoughts and writings of Adam Smith, Friedrich Hayek, Jonah Goldberg, and Zhang Weiying have shaped my worldview today. In particular, Professor Zhang Weiying's economic insights and courage in expressing his thoughts on free market economy have been a source of admiration and my greatest encouragement in writing.

I would like to extend my sincere thanks to Professor Chia-Wei Kuo, Dean for School of Professional Education and Continuing Studies at the National Taiwan University, for his contribution of the foreword to this book. From 2015 to 2017, during my time in the Global MBA program at NTU, Professor Kuo was my thesis advisor. His support during two pivotal moments in my life has been invaluable, and I am deeply appreciative of his help. Professor Kuo's concise and insightful writing not only captures the essence of this book but also reflects his profound insights on economics. His recognition has been the greatest encouragement for my continuous efforts and a significant honor in my creative journey. Professor Kuo's academic foundation and writing skills have been a lifelong inspiration to me.

I would like to express my gratitude to Maddie for her assistance with the editing process. Throughout the journey of writing, she has been a steadfast pillar of support. As a non-native English speaker, my work would undoubtedly have been lesser without her meticulous revisions. More importantly, her substantial encouragement and positive feedback have filled me with confidence in my writing. I am also deeply thankful for Karolina's professional cover design work.

I want to thank my dear friend Yuka, the first person who knew I was working on this book. Her encouragement and belief in me over the years have been the driving force behind my persistent efforts. I owe Eriko, for her professional advice on the cover design of this book. Her encouragement has been important to me. Her encouragements have been important to me. I am also deeply grateful to Christy at National Taiwan University for her tireless work in coordinating the promotion and preparation of this book at the university. Her support means the world to me, and I am truly touched by it. I would like to express my gratitude to my elementary school deskmates and friends, Shi Ruoqi (Sydney), and Xu Shiyu. Their encouragement and recognition of my writing have been a continuous source of motivation for me. We have known each other for over twenty years, the memories of our childhood spent learning and playing together remain vivid in my memory.

This book is dedicated for my late grandmother, Shen Jie. I was raised with her love and care since I was a child. From my earliest memories, she was the first person who ever spoke to me. My grandmother instilled in me the importance of sincerity and kindness, and as far back as I can remember, she never spoke to me harshly. Even when I made mistakes, she never scolded me; instead, she often offered comfort and encouragement. I attribute my wonderful childhood greatly to her influence, for which I am deeply grateful. But now, she has passed away. How I wish I could turn back time, just to have one more chance to express my gratitude and my love to her.

I want to thank my mother, Yuduan Yang, for her love, freedom, and sacrifices. These have been the driving forces behind my pursuit of dreams, and I can never fully repay her. The older I get, the more I realize that it is my mother's unconditional love and support that have allowed me to grow and thrive. Her strength and love are the most important pillars in my life. I am also deeply grateful to my father, Ran Fan Li, whose bold decision to leave China and venture abroad changed my destiny. The cover of this book features one of his oil paintings, a testament to the artistic talent I can only aspire to reach.

Finally, I want to express my deepest gratitude to my wife, Zoe. She is not just my beloved, but also my confidante and partner in brainstorming ideas. Her presence is felt in every part of this book. This book touches on philosophy in many places, a field I am deeply interested in but rarely write about. Whenever I doubted myself or lost my way, she was always there to give me the confidence I needed, reassuring me that I had the strength to overcome any obstacle. Like me, my wife also has a background in economics, and whenever I find myself in a mental impasse, she is always the first person I seek out for help. Her support has given me the courage to chase my dreams and face challenges with bravery. Having her as my wife is the greatest blessing of my life.

I do not expect this book to become a grand work, much less a masterpiece. My hope is simply that I have used all my abilities to craft clear, engaging, and vivid prose, conveying the ideas I wish to share. If this encourages the public to think more deeply and gain a better understanding of capitalism and the market economy, it would be a significant source of satisfaction for me.

Joe Zhankan Li

30th October 2024,
Frankfurt am Main, Germany

References

1. Beinhocker, Eric D, *The Origin of Wealth: The Radical Remaking of Economics and What it Means for Business and Society* (Harvard Business Review Press, Brighton, 2007).

2. Bremmer, Ian. *The End of the Free Market: Who Wins the War Between States and Corporations?* (Portfolio, London, 2010).

3. Butler, Eamonn. *Adam Smith: A Primer*, (Inst of Economic Affairs, London, 2007).

4. Butler, Eamonn. *Friedrich Hayek: The ideas and influence of the libertarian economist*, (Harriman House, Petersfield, 2012).

5. Butler, Eamonn. *Milton Friedman: A concise guide to the ideas and influence of the free-market economist*, (Harriman House, Petersfield, 2011).

6. Carter, Tim and Butt, John. *The Cambridge History of Seventeenth-Century Music: Volume 1*, (Cambridge University Press, Cambridge, 2005).

7. Coase, Ronald. *The federal communications Commission*, (Journal of law and economics, 1959).

8. Deaton, Angus. *The Great Escape: Health, Wealth, and the Origins of Inequality*, (Princeton University Press, Princeton, 2013).

9. Dikötter, Frank. *Mao's Great Famine* (WALKER & CO, New York, 2011).

10. Freeman, Samuel. *Rawls* (The Routledge Philosophers, Oxfordshire, 2007).

11. Friedman, Milton. *Capitalism and Freedom* (Univ of Chicago Press, Chicago, 2020).

12. Fukuyama, Francis. *The End of History and the Last Man*, (Free Press, New York, 1992).

13. Goldberg, Jonah. *Suicide of the West: How the Rebirth of*

Tribalism, Populism, Nationalism, and Identity Politics is Destroying American, (Crown Forum, New York, 2018).

14. Greenspan, Alan. *The Age of Turbulence: Adventures in a New World,* (Penguin, New York, 2008).

15. Hayek, Friedrich. *Road to Serfdom,* (University of Chicago Press, Chicago, 1989).

16. Hayek, Friedrich. *The Fatal Conceit: The Errors of Socialism,* (University of Chicago Press, Chicago, 1988).

17. Hazlitt, Henry. *Economics in One Lesson: The Shortest and Surest Way to Understand Basic Economics,* (Crown Currency, New York, 1988).

18. Hoerber, Thomas. *Hayek vs Keynes: A Battle of Ideas,* (Reaktion Books, London, 2017).

19. Hunter, Lewis. *Where Keynes Went Wrong: And Why World Governments Keep Creating Inflation, Bubbles, and Busts?* (Hunter Lewis Foundation, Crozet, 2011).

20. Ip, Greg. *Foolproof: Why Safety Can Be Dangerous and How Danger Makes Us Safe* (Little, Brown and Company, Boston, 2015).

21. Ito, Joi. *Whiplash: How to Survive Our Faster Future* (Grand Central Publishing, New York, 2016).

22. Iwata, Kikuo. *The Future of Capitalism,* (Kobunsha, Tokyo, 021).

23. Keynes, John. *The General Theory of Employment, Interest and Money,* (Macmillan, London, 1936).

24. Kling, Arnold. *Specialization and Trade,* (Cato Institute, San Francisco, 2016).

25. Kishtainy, Niall. *A Little History of Economics (Little Histories),* (Yale University Press, New Haven, 2017).

26. Lavoie, Don. *National Economic Planning: What Is Left?* (Mercatus Center at George Mason University, Arlington, 2016).

27. Li, Joe Zhankan. *Analysis of Income Inequality: Globalization, Technological progress and Money Supply*, (China Times Publishing Co., Taipei, 2017).

28. Liu, Qing, *The Unresolved Moment: Western Thought in the Discourse of Modernity*, (Xinxing Publishing, Beijing, 2006).

29. Marcuse, Herbert. *One-Dimensional Man* (Beacon Press, Boston, 1964).

30. Marx, Karl. *Capital A Critical Analysis of Capitalistic Production* (1867).

31. Menger, Carl, *Principles of Economics*, (New York University Press, New York, 1981).

32. Mill, John Stuart. *Principles of Political Economy* (1849).

33. Miller, Chris. *Chip War: The Fight for the World's Most Critical Technology*, (Scribner, New York, 2022).

34. Mises, Ludwig von. *The Theory of Money and Credit* (Liberty Press, Indianapolis, 1980).

35. Mobius, Mark. *The Inflation Myth and the Wonderful World of Deflation*, (Wiley, New Jersey, 2021).

36. Noguchi, Yukio. *Post-Economic History: Where Did We Go Wrong?*, (Nikkei BP Marketing, Tokyo, 2019).

37. Norman, Jesse. *Adam Smith*, (Allen Lane., London, 2018).

38. Nozick, Robert. *Anarchy, State, and Utopia*, (Basic Books., New York, 1974).

39. Okun, Arthur. *Equality and Efficiency REV: The Big Tradeoff*, Brookings Institution Press., Washington, D.C, 2015).

40. Popper, Karl. *Objective Knowledge: An Evolutionary Approach*, (Oxford University Press, Oxford, 1972).

41. Popper, Karl. *Objective Knowledge: An Evolutionary Approach*, (Oxford University Press, Oxford, 1972).

42. Rawls, John. *A theory of Justice* (Belknap Press, Cambridge, 1971).

43. Reagon, Ronald. *An American Life*, (Simon & Schuster, New

York, 1990).

44. Reed, Lawrence W. *Excuse Me, Professor: Challenging the Myths of Progressivism*, (Regnery Publishing, Washington, D.C., 2015).

45. Sandelin, Bo and Trautwein, Hans-Micheal. *A Short History of Economic Thought*, (Routledge, Oxfordshire, 2014).

46. Satre, Paul. *Being and Nothingness*, (Philosophical Library, New York, 1956).

47. Satre, Paul. *Existentialism Is a Humanism*, (Methuen Publishing, North Yorkshire, 1948).

48. Skousen, Mark. *Vienna & Chicago, Friends or Foes? A Tale of Two Schools of Free-Market Economics*, (Regnery Capital, Washington, D.C, 2005).

49. Sowell, Thomas. *Economic Facts and Fallacies: Second Edition*, (Basic Books, New York, 2011).

50. Taylor, Timothy. *The Instant Economist: Everything You Need to Know About How the Economy Works*, (Plume, New York, 2012).

51. Thatcher, Margaret. *The Downing Street*, (HarperCollins, London, 1995).

52. Wapshott, Nicolas. *Keynes Hayek: The Clash that Defined Modern Economics*, (W. W. Norton & Company, New York, 2012).

53. Wapshott, Nicolas. *Ronald Reagon and Margaret Thatcher: A Political Marriage* (Sentinel, New York, 2007).

54. Varoufakis, Yanis. *Talking to my daughter about the Economy or, How Capitalism Works—and How it Fails* (Vintage, New York, 2019).

55. Xue, Zhaofeng. *General Knowledge of Economics* (Peking University Press, Beijing, 2015).

56. Zhang, Weiying. *Logic of Market Economics* (Shanghai People's Publishing House, Shanghai, 2012).

57. Zhang, Weiying. *Market and Government*(Northwest University Press, Xian, 2014)

Notes

[1] From 1978 and for three decades afterward, China moved from central planning and autarky to a market-oriented economy. The growth of the nonstate sector has been the driving force in China's development. James A. Dorn, "China's Post-1978 Economic Development and Entry into the Global Trading System", *Cato*, October 10, 2023, https://www.cato.org/publications/chinas-post-1978-economic-development-entry-global-trading-system

[2] Majority of young adults in US hold negative view of capitalism: poll, "Majority of young adults in US hold negative view of capitalism: poll" , Julia Manchester, *The Hill*, 28 June, 2021, https://thehill.com/homenews/campaign/560493-majority-of-young-adults-in-us-hold-negative-view-of-capitalism-poll/

[3] Eat the rich! Why millennials and generation Z have turned their backs on capitalism, Owen Jones, "Eat the rich! Why millennials and generation Z have turned their backs on capitalism", *The Guardian*, 20 September 2021, https://www.theguardian.com/politics/2021/sep/20/eat-the-rich-why-millennials-and-generation-z-have-turned-their-backs-on-capitalism

[4] Majority of young adults in US hold negative view of capitalism: poll, "Majority of young adults in US hold negative view of capitalism: poll" , Julia Manchester, *The Hill*, 28 June, 2021, https://thehill.com/homenews/campaign/560493-majority-of-young-adults-in-us-hold-negative-view-of-capitalism-poll/

[5] Definition of Humanism; IHEU (1996) IHEU Minimum Statement on Humanism. Humanists International, General Assembly.

[6] Carter, Tim and Butt, John. *The Cambridge History of Seventeenth Century Music: Volume 1,* (Cambridge University Press, Cambridge, 2005) p. 4.

[7] For example, in the Western Middle Ages, people believed that one had to live according to religious doctrines in order to attain heaven. The Bible served as the definitive guide for all moral goodness. However, these beliefs gradually lost authority after the Renaissance.

[8] Conrad, Sebastian (1 October 2012). "Enlightenment in Global History: A Historiographical Critique". The American Historical Review. P.117.

[9] Butler, Eamonn. *Adam Smith: A Primer*, (Inst of Economic Affairs, London, 2007). p.2.

[10] *Ibid.*

[11] Definition of Supply and Demand Relationship: The model of demand and supply are fundamental concepts in economics. Demand refers to the purchasing requirements generated by consumers who need a product, while supply refers to the products provided by businesses in response to consumer demand. When demand exceeds supply (scarcity), prices tend to rise, and when supply exceeds demand (discount promotions), prices tend to fall; Taylor, Timothy. *The Instant Economist: Everything You Need to Know About How the Economy Works*, (Plume, New York, 2012). P.12

[12] In the late 1970s, after the "Chinese Reform", the government reformed its economic operations to employ market-oriented methods. However, China has never acknowledged having a capitalist system. Theoretically, China is a "socialist" country with Chinese characteristics, but in practice, China has few socialist elements, and its system does not differ significantly from that of capitalist countries. Stephen McDonell, "Changing China: Xi Jinping's effort to return to socialism", *BBC*, 23 September, 2021, https://www.bbc.com/news/business-58579831

[13] Varoufakis, Yanis. *Talking to my daughter about the Economy or, How Capitalism Works—and How it Fails* (Vintage, New York, 2019).

[14] Maslow, Abraham H. (1943). "A theory of human motivation". Psychological Review.

[15] The rise of ancient civilizations such as Chinese civilization, Mesopotamian civilization, and Egyptian civilization was closely related to highly developed agriculture. Ancient Greece, however, was a major exception.

[16] Lavoie, Don. *National Economic Planning: What Is Left?* (Mercatus Center at George Mason University, Arlington, 2016) p.13

[17] Mass-Energy Equivalence, $E = mc^2$, https://plato.stanford.edu/entries/equivME/

[18] Maxwell's equations, (1) div D = ρ, (2) div B = 0, (3) curl E = -dB/dt, and (4) curl H = dD/dt + J, https://www.maxwells-equations.com/

[19] More about Psychoanalysis, Kendra Cherry, "How Psychoanalysis Influenced the Field of Psychology", *Verywellmind*, May 05, 2023, https://www.verywellmind.com/what-is-psychoanalysis-2795246

[20] *Laissez-faire* refers to an economic theory or plan in which a government does not have many laws or rules to control the buying and selling of goods and services.

[21] Sandelin, Bo and Trautwein, Hans-Micheal. *A Short History of Economic Thought,* (Routledge, Oxfordshire, 2014) p.35

[22] Idem, p.87.

[23] Taylor, Timothy. *The Instant Economist: Everything You Need to Know About How the Economy Works*, (Plume, New York, 2012) p.201.

[24] Idem, p.170.

[25] About critical rationalism: Popper, Karl. *The Logic of Scientific Discovery (2nd English ed.)*. (New York, NY: Routledge Classics, 1959).

[26] Dikötter, Frank. Mao's Great Famine (WALKER & CO, New York, 2011).

[27] Bremmer, Ian. *The End of the Free Market: Who Wins the War Between States and Corporations?* (Portfolio, London, 2010) p.77-78.

[28] The Phillips Curve posits that there is a negative correlation between inflation and the unemployment rate, implying that stimulating inflation can boost employment and economic prosperity; Taylor, Timothy. *The Instant Economist: Everything You Need to Know About How the Economy Works,* (Plume, New York, 2012) p.157-159.

[29] Definition of Stagnation◇Taylor, Timothy. *The Instant Economist: Everything You Need to Know About How the Economy Works*, (Plume, New York, 2012) p141.

[30] Hyperinflation is a type of uncontrolled inflation in which, as prices rapidly increase, the currency also loses its value. Taylor, Timothy. *The Instant Economist: Everything You Need to Know About How the Economy Works*, (Plume, New York, 2012) p141.

[31]Imported inflation refers to the phenomenon where the continuous rise in domestic prices is caused by the increase in prices of foreign goods or production factors. Vincent Launay, "Definition of imported inflation", *Central Charts*, 25 March, 2015, https://www.centralcharts.com/en/gm/1-learn/9-economics/34-fundamental-analysis/946-definition-imported-inflation

[32] The purpose of the Plaza Accord was to jointly intervene in the foreign exchange market to orderly devalue the U.S. dollar against major currencies such as the Japanese yen and the German mark, in order to address the United States' large trade deficit. Since the U.S. dollar was already the currency used for international transactions at that time, the exchange rate fluctuations caused by the trade deficit were not beneficial to any country. Iwata, Kikuo. *The future of Capitalism,* (Kobunsha, Tokyo, 2021) p.201.

[33] The phrase "Japan's Lost Decade" refers to the period following the burst of Japan's economic bubble, during which the Japanese economy experienced prolonged

deflation and low economic growth◈ Noguchi, Yukio. *Post-Economic History: Where Did We Go Wrong?*, (Nikkei BP Marketing, Tokyo, 2019) p.264.

[34] The purpose of developing an economy should be the happiness and well-being of the citizens, with economic interventions and policy serving merely as the means to that end. However, in practice, planned and mixed economies often mistake these means for the ultimate goals.

[35] Taylor, Timothy. *The Instant Economist: Everything You Need to Know About How the Economy Works*, (Plume, New York, 2012) p.119.

[36] Zhang, Weiying. *Market and Government* (Northwest University Press, Xian, 2014) p.395.

[37] Quantitative easing is a monetary policy implemented by central banks of various countries, aimed at injecting funds into the market to stimulate the economy. Taylor, Timothy. The Instant Economist: Everything You Need to Know About How the Economy Works, (Plume, New York, 2012) p195.

[38] Li, Joe Zhankan. *Analysis of Income Inequality◈Globalization, Technological progress and Money Supply*, (China Times Publishing Co., Taipei, 2017).

[39] Inflation occurs when the supply of money in the economy increases faster than the supply of goods and services. When people have more money to spend but the availability of products remains the same, demand rises. Businesses respond by raising their prices since they know customers are willing to pay more. This overall increase in prices leads to inflation.

[40] Because when newly printed money is introduced into the market as loans, it is often the wealthy or asset-rich individuals who are prioritized in obtaining these loans. For banks, lending to them carries lower risk.

[41] Several assumptions of modern economic theory include that everyone is equally and completely rational, the economy has no externalities, there are decreasing returns to scale, information is fully symmetric, and competition is sufficient and perfect, among others; Zhang, Weiying. *Market and Government* (Northwest University Press, Xian, 2014) p.12-13.

[42] Even in the 21st century, the principle that supply drives demand remains true for the development of microchips. When microchips were first invented, no one knew exactly how they would be applied in real life. The specific uses and demand for this new invention were discovered only after its creation; Miller, Chris. Chip War: The Fight for the World's Most Critical Technology, (Scribner, New York, 2022).

[43] Hayek, Friedrich. *The Fatal Conceit: The Errors of Socialism*, (University of Chicago Press, Chicago, 1988).

[44] Ip, Greg. *Foolproof: Why Safety Can Be Dangerous and How Danger Makes Us Safe* (Little, Brown and Company, Boston, 2015), . p.19.

[45] Planned economies have caused severe issues in several communist countries, including shortages of goods, economic collapse, and famines, leading to significant human suffering. Mila, "The 'planned economy' ultimately led to the collapse of the Soviet regime, and the Chinese Communist Party is following the same old path.", *The News Lens*, June 21, 2021, https://www.thenewslens.com/article/152468

[46] Lavoie, Don. National Economic Planning: What Is Left? (Mercatus Center at George Mason University, Arlington, 2016), p.30.

[47] Kling, Arnold. Specialization and Trade, (Cato Institute, San Francisco, 2016), p.95.

[48] Transaction costs are expenses incurred when buying or selling a good or service, outside the cost of the good or service itself. Brian Mitchell, "Buy-side Firms Use TCA to Measure Execution Performance", *Global Trading*, June 10, 2010, https://www.fixglobal.com/home/buy-side-firms-use-tca-to-measure-execution-performance/

[49] Wapshott, Nicolas. *Keynes Hayek: The Clash that Defined Modern Economics,* (W. W. Norton & Company, New York, 2012) p.243.

[50] Fukuyama, Francis. *The End of History and the Last Man,* (Free Press, New York, 1992).

[51] The 1929 global economic crisis reached Germany, leading to the collapse and recession of its aid-dependent economy. The government responded by drastically cutting spending and raising taxes to stimulate growth. Expecting the crisis to end soon and that recovery would follow, the government also printed a substantial amount of money to address its deficits, causing severe hyperinflation., History.com Editors, "Weimar Republic", *History.com*, September 21, 2022, https://www.history.com/topics/european-history/weimar-republic

[52] The New Deal denotes the range of economic policies enacted by President Franklin D. Roosevelt upon taking office in 1933, emphasizing active government intervention. History.com Editors, "New Deal", *History.com*, March 28, 2023, https://www.history.com/topics/great-depression/new-deal

[53] Friedman, Milton. Capitalism and Freedom (Univ of Chicago Press, Chicago, 2020)

[54] The World Bank Data, https://data.worldbank.org/

[55] Marcuse, Herbert. *One-Dimensional Man* (Beacon Press, Boston, 1964)

[56] Lydia Saad, "Socialism as Popular as Capitalism Among Young Adults in U.S.", *Gallup*, November 25, 2019, https://news.gallup.com/poll/268766/socialism-popular-capitalism-among-young-adults.aspx

[57] Traveling with an airplane was once a luxury in the 1960s, Valerie Forgeard, "When Flying Was a Luxury: Airfare Prices in the 1960s", *Brilliantio*, June 23, 2023, https://brilliantio.com/how-much-were-plane-tickets-in-the-1960s

[58] Zhang, Weiying. *Logic of Market Economics* (Shanghai People's Publishing House, Shanghai, 2012) p.49

[59] From 1962 to 1979, the Chinese central government mandated the temporary resettlement of roughly 18 million urban youths to rural areas across the country. The movement's coercive features, together with strict restrictions on migration during that period, provide an ideal natural experiment to identify the causal impact of the better-educated sent-down youths (SDYs) on the less-educated local rural residents. Yi Chen et al, "Arrival of Young Talents: The Send-down Movement and Rural Education in China", *ECONSTOR*, 2018, https://www.econstor.eu/handle/10419/183616

[60] Taylor, Timothy. *The Instant Economist: Everything You Need to Know About How the Economy Works,* (Plume, New York, 2012) p.12

[61] Nozick, Robert. *Anarchy, State, and Utopia,* (Basic Books., New York, 1974)

[62] S. Marc Cohen, "The allegory of cave" , *University of Washington*, 2006, https://faculty.washington.edu/smcohen/320/cave.htm

[63] Rawls, John. A theory of Justice (Belknap Press, Cambridge, 1971)

[64] Nozick, Robert. *Anarchy, State, and Utopia,* (Basic Books., New York, 1974).

[65] Idem,

[66] Robert Siegel, "Those who give up essential liberty to purchase a little temporary safety, deserve neither liberty nor safety.", *npr*, March 2, 2015, https://www.npr.org/2015/03/02/390245038/ben-franklins-famous-liberty-safety-quote-lost-its-context-in-21st-century

[67] Hayek, Friedrich. *The Fatal Conceit: The Errors of Socialism,* (University of Chicago Press, Chicago, 1988).

[68] Kishtainy, Niall. *A Little History of Economics (Little Histories),* (Yale University Press, New Haven, 2017) p.79.

[69] Lavoie, Don. *National Economic Planning: What Is Left?* (Mercatus Center at George Mason University, Arlington, 2016) p.86

[70] Tacit Knowledge. Indeed Editorial Team, "What Is Tacit Knowledge? Definition, Examples and Importance", *indeed*, August 16, 2024, https://www.indeed.com/career-advice/career-development/tacit-knowledge-example

[71] Hayek, Friedrich. *Road to Serfdom,* (University of Chicago Press, Chicago, 1989)

[72] Machine learning, Lev Craig , "What is machine learning? Guide, definition and examples", *TechTarget*, August 2024, https://www.techtarget.com/searchenterpriseai/definition/machine-learning-ML

[73] Amanda Hetler , "What is ChatGPT", *TechTarget*, July 2024, https://www.techtarget.com/whatis/definition/ChatGPT

[74] Ito, Joi. *Whiplash: How to Survive Our Faster Future* (Grand Central Publishing, New York, 2016) p.37

[75] Wapshott, Nicolas. *Ronald Reagon and Margaret Thatcher: A Political Marriage* (Sentinel, New York, 2007).

[76] The 2008 stimulus package announced by China's then premier, Wen Jiabao, after the 2008 financial crisis. Ji Siqi, "Who makes China's stimulus decisions, and what's the procedure?", *South China Morning Post*, October 14, 2024, https://www.scmp.com/economy/policy/article/3282326/who-makes-chinas-stimulus-decisions-and-whats-procedure

[77] The Nordic Model, James McWhinney, "The Nordic Model: Pros and Cons", *Investopia*, October 02, 2023, https://www.investopedia.com/articles/investing/100714/nordic-model-pros-and-cons.asp

[78] Pareto Principle, Robert Kelly, " What Is the Pareto Principle—aka the Pareto Rule or 80/20 Rule?", *Investopia*, June 27, 2024, https://www.investopedia.com/terms/p/paretoprinciple.asp

[79] "Many forms of Government have been tried, and will be tried in this world of sin and woe. No one pretends that democracy is perfect or all-wise. Indeed it has been said that democracy is the worst form of Government except for all those other forms that have been tried from time to time...."

[80] Marx, Karl. *A Contribution to the Critique of Political Economy*. (Intl Pub Co Inc, New York, 1977) https://www.marxists.org/archive/marx/works/1859/critique-pol-economy/preface.htm

[81] Idem,

[82] Lavoie, Don. *National Economic Planning: What Is Left?* (Mercatus Center at George Mason University, Arlington, 2016) p.18.

[83] "From each according to his abilities, to each according to his needs", Richard Fulmer, "Socialists' Claims About Socialism", *Econlib*, 2022, https://www.econlib.org/socialists-claims-about-socialism/